Your Fate and Future Are Written on Your Face

The Chinese have been reading faces for more than 3,000 years. Now, with this extensive pictorial guide, you can learn to use this fascinating form of divination to decode the secrets of fate—for yourself, your loved ones, even complete strangers!

In this comprehensive handbook, you'll learn to analyze each feature of the face—its complexion and shape, the eyes, cheekbones, and mouth—and what they mean in terms of wealth, romance, career success, health, and family life. You'll also discover how the principles of harmony and balance, yin and yang, and the five elements are applied in Chinese face reading.

From understanding what a resemblance to a specific animal means, to mastering a little-known shortcut to face reading, the knowledge you'll gain from *What Your Face Reveals* will enable you determine the personality of strangers, uncover your future and the future of your loved ones, and use this knowledge to benefit you in work, health, and love.

About the Author

Henry B. Lin is a third generation master in the ancient Chinese art of face reading. He has been practicing face reading for more than two decades. His service is characterized by astonishing accuracy in the description of the past and the prediction of the future with regard to one's personality, career, health, relationships, family, and wealth. Lin resides in Seattle, Washington and has written several articles on face reading, feng shui, and other divination topics in local publications such as *Seattle Chinese News* and *The New Times*.

To Write to the Author

If you wish to contact the author or would like more information about this book, please write to the author in care of Llewellyn Worldwide, and we will forward your request. Both the author and publisher appreciate hearing from you. Llewellyn Worldwide cannot guarantee that every letter written to the author can be answered, but all will be forwarded. Please write to:

Henry B. Lin
℅ Llewellyn Worldwide
P.O. Box 64383, Dept. K433-2
St. Paul, MN 55164-0383, U.S.A.

Please enclose a self-addressed, stamped envelope for reply, or $1.00 to cover costs.
If outside the U.S.A., enclose international postal reply coupon.

What Your Face Reveals

CHINESE SECRETS OF FACE READING

Henry B. Lin

Foreword by Richard Webster

1999
Llewellyn Publications
Saint Paul, Minnesota 55164-0383, U.S.A.

FIRST EDITION
First printing, 1999

Cover design: Lisa Novak
Front and back cover photographs: Digital Vision
Illustrations: Carrie Westfall
Interior photos: Associated Press
Editing and book design: Christine Nell Snow
Editorial consultant: Richard Webster

Library of Congress Cataloging-in-Publication Data
Lin, Henry B., 1955–
      What your face reveals: Chinese secrets of face reading / Henry B. Lin; foreword by Richard Webster. — 1st ed.
         p. cm.
      Includes bibliographical references and index.
      ISBN 1-56718-433-2
      1. Physiognomy–China. I. Title.
    BF851.L56 1999
    138'.0951—dc21

99-11653
CIP

Llewellyn Publications
A Division of Llewellyn Worldwide, Ltd.
P.O. Box 64383, Dept. K433-2
St. Paul, MN 55164-0383

 Printed in the United States of America on recycled paper

Dedication

To my parents who gave me a face . . .
and to my teachers who taught me how to read it.

Forthcoming Books From the Author

Chinese Health Care Secrets: A Natural Lifestyle Approach (Llewellyn, 2000)

Contents

Tables

福 Foreword

People have always been fascinated with faces and their changing moods and expressions. It is not surprising that physiognomy, the ancient art of reading someone's character from their outward appearance, came into existence. In China, the art of face reading was known as *siang mien*, and was used to determine a person's past, present, and future.

The art probably began in China and is still extremely popular throughout the Far East. King Solomon remarked that the heart of a man is open to the eyes of a wise man. The ancient Greeks were fascinated with physiognomy and related different types of faces to various animals and their characteristics. Aristotle was vitally interested in the subject and did a great deal to increase its popularity in the West. William Shakespeare was obviously aware of the subject and made many intriguing references to the face. For instance, in *Macbeth*, his character Duncan says: "There's no art to find the mind's construction in the face." Goethe contributed a chapter to a book on physiognomy by his friend, Johann Kaspar Lavater, who was largely responsible for the nineteenth-century Western revival of interest in the subject. Charles Darwin was fascinated with what he called "the discovery of the disposition of the mind by the lineaments of the body." In the days of silent movies, facial expressions and gestures had to be exaggerated to ensure that everyone in the audience understood what was going on. This created further interest in the subject. In contemporary China, both Chiang Kaishek and Mao Tse-tung were known to have utilized face readers.

Whether or not we are are aware of it, we are reading facial expressions every time we look at someone. Even small babies quickly learn to interpret the expressions in their parents' faces, and we continue to make decisions based on what we read in the faces of others for the rest of our lives. We commonly judge people from their facial expressions without even realizing that we are doing so. We might say that someone has "shifty eyes" or has an "open face." In making these assessments, we are intuitively reading the person's face.

It has been pointed out that our faces are simply a result of heredity, and consequently, it is impossible to determine character by simply looking at someone's face. However, we are born with a number of potentials, including our personalities and talents, in the same way that we are born with a certain physique and facial features. As we progress through life, these inborn characteristics become more and more visible through our faces. A photographer friend of mine says that she particularly loves photographing older people, as their faces have developed character. Of course, everyone's face shows character, but it is easier to read and photograph older people. Emotions are readily visible in the face, and our character is also easily read by anyone who is skilled in physiognomy.

Henry Lin has spent a lifetime researching and studying the ancient Chinese art of face reading. People all around the world attest to his skill and accuracy at reading their past, present, and futures in their faces. His knowledge and enthusiasm brings face reading to life and his book provides the perfect introduction to the subject.

You are already reading faces everywhere you go. With the help of this book, you will be able to read faces with much more accuracy and gain enormous insight into other people's motivations. This will help you enormously as you progress through life.

—Richard Webster

福 Preface

Believe it or not, your fate is written on your face. Appearance can be reality. For thousands of years, masters of face reading in China have relied on the outward appearances of their clients, reading their facial structures, shapes, and features to accurately predict their fate in terms of wealth, relationships, career, health, family, travel, and more.

Indeed, there is much more to be seen in a face than what ordinarily meets the eyes, including your own. In fact, your face is not just your appearance; it is a significant indicator of what you are, what you have been, and what you will be. It is altogether fitting to regard beauty as only skin deep, but it is painfully wrong to dismiss individual facial structures and features as nothing more than superficial marks.

There is a whole world of secret and precious information written on your face. Of course, it is written in a special language, and it takes special training to decode it. Until now, only a few could claim to having mastered that special language, although the language itself has been in existence for thousands of years in China. Part of the reason for this is because the art of face reading has been regarded as a top secret, guarded with intense jealousy by those who understand it.

Face reading is one of the oldest professions in China. Ever since the dawn of Chinese civilization, the Chinese have constantly sought advice and guidance from face readers and other kinds of fortunetellers to help them make important decisions in life. This is especially true for those in power, such as emperors. The underlying belief is that every one of us is born with a fate controlled by supernatural agents and written in different languages, all of them mysterious and in need of expert decoding to make practical sense. Face reading, astrology, and palmistry are three major languages in which one's fate is written.

The reason for man's obsession with learning his fate is not hard to understand. As humans, we are naturally curious about what exactly is waiting ahead for us—and the sooner we know it, the better. This information can be an invaluable aid in the strategic planning of our lives, so that we know what to do and when. Knowing when to take advantage of a situation or what to avoid can save us a lot of time, energy, money, and humiliation. For example, if you know beforehand that you are not meant to be rich in this lifetime, you can stop wasting your efforts and learn to take financial misfortune with greater composure, maybe even laugh it away. Instead you can spend your very limited time, energy, and money on something more realistic for you, such as concentrating on your health, increasing your knowledge, or at least staying away from gambling or playing the stock market. As another example, if you know beforehand that you were not born to be a successful business person, but can climb high up the ladder of a military career, it can make the decision process much easier when it comes time to decide which school to go to or what kind of jobs to seek.

There definitely seems to be a supernatural force that determines our individual course in life the moment we are born. The disappointing fact is that humans are not born equal—not in ability, intelligence, physique, and, least of all, in wealth and family happiness, despite all the democratic claims to the contrary. Thus, some people can go a long way in their careers and relationships without much effort. Others, however, do not make a lot of progress in those areas, even with a lot of effort. One can, during a certain period of time, basically work oneself to death, but still fall short of success; whereas in other times, the same person can achieve a lot more with much less labor. In other words, the same person can, and most likely has, a different fate in different times. For instance, Bill Clinton could not have become president of the United States before 1992, no matter how hard he might have tried, nor would he have so much political, personal, and financial trouble before 1998 as he has today (all because his forehead isn't very auspicious).

This is individual fate working at different times, otherwise known as "yun" or the five-year period in Chinese fortunetelling. While fate refers to the fortune of one's entire life, yun refers to the fate in a specific five-year period. In terms of face reading, the concept of yun is represented by individual facial features as well as the color and spirit of a face during a specific age. Thus, a person can have an auspicious forehead but a terribly unlucky nose. This facial information says that the person must have been very happy as a child but will be miserable in their middle age.

A common belief is that Communists do not believe in fate or God. This cannot be further from the truth. Mao Tse-tung (1893–1976), a great Chinese leader, was a profound believer in fate. He used to throw I Ching coins as an aid in making strategic decisions. It is said that as he toured the country, he liked to visit temples high in famous mountains and draw lots there to help him solve problems. Perhaps most illustrative of his belief in fate is the following fact: During his later years in the 1970s, Mao liked to recite to visiting foreign heads of state the famous Chinese saying, "At the age of seventy-three or eighty-four, one will most likely go to see the Head of the Hell voluntarily without even being invited by the latter." As if to verify his foresight, he died at the age of eighty-four (by traditional Chinese calculation, a person is counted as one year old at the time of birth).

Not only do individual humans have different fates, nations and ethnic groups have different fates, too. For instance, the birth of Adolph Hitler dramatically changed the fortune of not only the German nation, but also that of the entire world. This event had been accurately projected by some fortunetellers long before Hitler came to power. More fascinating is the fact that great Chinese fortunetellers such as Jiang Taigong, Zhu Geliang the master mind, and Liu Ji, who lived thousands of years ago, were able to accurately predict the timing and personages responsible for the rise and fall of different dynasties yet to come, to the surprise of later generations. These predictions are well documented in books written by Zhu Geliang, Liu Ji, and Jiang Luwang (see Bibliography). Read these books and you will be surprised to know how logically things are predetermined by supernatural forces beyond our power to understand.

What, then, accounts for wide differences in individual fate? Reasons may vary depending on events, but in the final analysis, it is our own behavior and performance in a prior life that makes the difference. Ancient Chinese believe in reincarnation, which means the recycling of an individual from one lifetime to another. They hold that most people have lived a prior life before the current one. This reincarnation is controlled by God, who keeps an accurate record of what we have done in our lifetime to determine what our next lifetime will be. Thus, if you have done a lot of good deeds, such as helping people, and led a moralistic life, you are bound to be rewarded with good luck in your next life. On the other hand, if you are corrupt or greedy in this life, living a decadent lifestyle, you are destined to be punished with bad luck in your next life. This is based on the Chinese thinking that God has longer arms than justice.

We all know that comparisons are odious, but not many of us know that comparisons can also be cancerous and even suicidal. Comparing what we have with what luckier ones have may lead to stress, depression, illness, premature death, and even suicide. Perhaps the Chinese are most aware of this fact of life. Confucius solemnly declared

to the world: "It is impossible to be a high-virtue person without knowing one's own fate." He himself is an excellent example of such a good-virtued person. Hard-pressed by poverty and having his political ambitions thwarted most of the time, Confucius remained an undaunted, optimistic, and upright sage. He told his disciples: "If wealth can be sought by human means, I would be willing to be a cart driver for others." For a great sage to become a cart driver was a tremendous condescension. Of course, the meaning behind his statement is this: wealth is predetermined by fate; all efforts to change it will be to little avail.

As the ruling elite of Chinese society, Confucians rely heavily on the concept of fate to steel themselves in the face of crisis, to help them resolve conflict, and to console them against disillusions in life situations. However, they do not completely resign themselves to fate. They hold that the right outlook toward life is based on the balance between predetermined fate and human diligence. This attitude is most evident in the Confucian teaching: "Do your best and resign the rest to fate."

Can fate, then, really be known and foretold? Certainly it can, but it takes special tools because the secrets of fortune are written in special languages—the language of the hand (palmistry), the language of birthdays (astrology/numerology), and the language of faces (face reading). Decoding the secrets of fortune is called "divination." Chinese divination uses tools to induce supernatural forces to reveal the secrets in the course of human affairs and that of nature. It is an important means by which people obtain valuable guidance as to what actions to take at a time of confusion, or to gain confidence at a time of distress, or to find consolation when misfortune hits.

As an elder member in the mysterious family of Chinese divination, face reading contains a very unique value as compared with other methods of divination such as astrology, palmistry, and numerology. The great advantage of face reading lies in that it requires no cooperation, not even consent, on the part of the person being read. The face is the most obvious part of a person (with perhaps the exception of those who choose to cover up their faces in public). So long as the face is shown, a master of face reading will be able to see through this "window" and tell the inside story about the person and his or her family.

As such, face reading provides us with a very convenient and powerful tool to reveal the secrets of the fortune and personality of ourselves and others whom we may not even know. As the world becomes more and more integrated, and contact with others becomes increasingly frequent and important, the art of face divination can be of tremendous help in your decision making and interpersonal skills regarding hiring and promotion, making friends, establishing relationships, finding a spouse, or selecting business partners.

As will be revealed in this book, Chinese face reading takes into consideration all aspects of the face—from individual features to facial color, from age to location, from proportion to spirit. It is the holistic, combined evaluation of all these factors, both visible and invisible, that makes face reading a profound art in the truest sense of the word, taking years of experience to master. So do not expect to become an expert right away. Some of the material may be more difficult to understand and apply than other material. Just be patient and keep practicing.

Remember that the interpretations and fates revealed by the facial features tell of events that are *most likely* to happen or have happened, and are not necessarily as inevitable as they may sound.

It is also important to note that colors or features designated as "normal" or "auspicious" given throughout this book are based on the norms of the Chinese culture. Modern face readers should take into account the ethnic background of the person being read to determine what color or feature is considered the norm for that ethnicity. This is a very complicated issue on which no Chinese face reading book has ever touched, nor have I made a good study of. Widespread intermarriages between people of different ethnic backgrounds only increases that complexity. The only thing that I can contribute at this point is to warn people that all conclusions drawn here are strictly Chinese, so adjustments will need to be made based on each person's ethnic background.

The process for reading a face is basically the same as the order of the chapters in this book. You'll first learn important principles and perspectives that define and guide the art as well as a little-known shortcut to get a broad summary of someone's fate. Then you'll progress into the individual facial features that are listed in chronological order, beginning with the first years in life (ears) all the way to old age (facial bones). Numerous illustrations accompany most chapters to help you visualize the specific features described. Look for reference tables at the end of chapters which briefly summarize the criteria you need to look for in a particular feature. Sample face readings of well-known world figures are placed throughout the book to help you apply your knowledge and match it against my interpretations. The last chapter contains a convenient list of tips to keep in mind as you practice your art.

The three appendices contain additional information for those interested. Appendix A discusses man-animal resemblance and how looking similar to a certain type of animal can indicate your fate. Appendices B and C focus on the highly traditional aspects of males and females, detailing the specific features and characteristics that many Chinese looked for in a spouse, and some still do today.

Face reading itself can be a very subjective art, as is the case with almost all other kinds of arts. That is why different readers can come up with very different readings regarding the fate of the same person. That is what makes art an art.

To learn this ancient Chinese art is at once challenging, interesting, and rewarding. It is the purpose of this book to help you meaningfully read faces so you can come up with insightful and valuable conclusions about the fate and fortune in your own life and those around you.

—Henry B. Lin

Chapter 1

A Brief History of Chinese Face Reading

The art of looking at, and interpreting, the facial features of animals and humans is considered one of the great inventions of the ancient Chinese. The study of people's facial characteristics and relating it to their fate can be dated back almost to the very beginning of Chinese civilization. Some of the earliest recordings say that Emperor Yao, one of the earliest rulers in ancient China and the third successor to the Yellow Emperor (2697–2577 B.C.), had a pair of eyebrows that shined like a rainbow. Another emperor at that time, named Yu, is said to have had three holes in each of his ears. King Wen, the father of the Zhou Dynasty, is said to have had four nipples in his breast. All these unusual features are interpreted as indicators of emperors. Emperor Sun, Emperor Yao's successor, was born with two dark pupils in each eye. This is interpreted by Chinese physiognomy, or face reading, as a sure sign of the Mandate of Heaven, i.e., the mission given by God for someone to rule a country. We are told by Si Maqian, one of the greatest historians and authors in ancient China, that the King of Chu, who lived in the third century B.C. also had double pupils.

The King of Chu's political enemy was Liu Bang, the founder of the Han Dynasty (206 B.C.–A.D. 220). Liu possessed some extraordinary facial and body characteristics. Si Maqian found that Liu had a nose like that of a dragon—high, straight, long, and fleshy—and had seventy-two black moles on his left leg. As Liu was still a common man, he liked to drink a lot, often in a "bar" close to where he lived. Each time he drank during the day, he fell. At these times, the owner of the establishment could see a real golden dragon lingering in the sky directly above Liu. As Liu woke up, the dragon disappeared. This convinced the owner that Liu would become an emperor, and he acted quickly and decisively to propose and arrange the marriage between Liu and his only beautiful daughter. This was a great blessing for poor Liu, who could not otherwise afford a wife at that time, let alone a beautiful one.

As early as the Warring States Period (481–221 B.C.), a Taoist immortal with the nickname of Gui Gu-Tze, or literally, "the Master of the Demon Gorge," was famous for reading faces. Gui Gu-Tze is today widely regarded as the father of Chinese face reading.

The story goes that one day Gui Gu-Tze was summoned by the emperor of Qi State to advise him on a planned military expedition against a neighboring state. Without revealing to Gui Gu-Tze any details of his strategy, the emperor asked the master face reader to predict the outcome of his campaign. After gazing at the emperor for a few moments, Gui Gu-Tze warned the emperor of some serious personal danger that would occur if the war was to be started within a week, as was planned by the emperor. The emperor was so impatient and furious with his enemy, and so convinced of his superiority in strength that he dismissed the advice of the face reader. He went ahead with the military campaign nonetheless. The result was a total defeat of the emperor's army. During the battle, the emperor received a poisonous arrow in his chest, and died a week later.

Although he is known as the father of physiognomy, Gui Gu-Tze was not the first master of face divination in China. His reputation comes largely from his book *Xiang Bian Wei Mang*, or literally, "A Detailed Analysis of Face." It is the first classic book on the art of face reading that is still in existence. I remember the moment when my Chinese teacher of face reading adopted me as his student. In a solemn ceremony, we all bowed to the altar and the idol of Gui Gu-Tze as an introduction to the serious subject of physiognomy. It is interesting to note that this master of face divination was also a great educator and philosopher. He had two famous students—one became a great general while the other became a famous prime minister. Sun Bin, the author of *The Art of War of Sun Bin* became a general, and Pang Juan ultimately became prime minister. They were two of his best students who later became deadly enemies for political reasons.

After Gui Gu-Tze, many other master readers made lasting contributions to physiognomy. Among the more significant ones are Xu Fu of the Western Han Dynasty (202 B.C.–A.D. 18), who wrote *Xiang De Qi Di Wu* or "Relations between Morality and Face"; Guo Linzhong of the Eastern Han Dynasty (19–A.D. 220) who wrote *Face Divination and the Five Elements*; and Guan Chi and Zhang Zhongyuan, who were famous face readers in the Three Kingdom Period (A.D. 221–265). The famous Taoist immortal Lu Dongbin of the Tang Dynasty (A.D. 618–907) made his permanent mark on the art of physiognomy with his book *Introduction to Face Divination.*

In the early Tang dynasty, there was a great Taoist named Yuan Tiangang from Chendu in Sichuan province. He was famous for his skills in revealing the fortunes of individuals and even the entire nation. Yuan is the author of *Pictures of Pushing the Back*, which is a wonderful sealed book (a book written largely in puns, the decoding of which takes great skill, and its meanings usually become clear only after the historical events alluded to have occurred) revealing the fate of China during the Tang dynasty (A.D. 618–907) to well into the future. Up to this day, all of his predictions and descriptions regarding the major events in the past fourteen centuries have come true. These predictions and descriptions are mainly of major events in China, but occasionally international events have been predicted. For instance, the book accurately predicted the usurpation of the throne by the second son of emperor Zhu Yuanzhang of the Ming dynasty, the consequent shifting of the Ming capital from Nanjing to Peking, the Manchurian rule of China proper, and the revolution of 1911, which led to the collapse of the Manchurian regime.

There are many legends attached to Yuan Tiangang. One story goes that Yuan Tiangang was invited to the home of Li Yuan, who was a powerful general stationed in the capital city of Shanxi Province in northern China. He had heard of Yuan's fame as a master face reader. After briefly commenting on the face of Li Yuan, Yuan Tiangang turned around to gaze at Li's second son, Li Shimin, who was then only thirteen years old. Yuan Tiangang told Li Yuan: "Shimin's appearance combines the features of a dragon and a phoenix. I am sure he will be able to save the country and the Chinese people at the age of twenty." Several years later at the age of twenty, Li Shimin led a victorious army that conquered the country. After killing his two brothers, he succeeded to the throne and named his empire the Tang Dynasty.

After Li Shimin became emperor, he enthusiastically invited Yuan Tiangang to the palace to visit. Among the hundreds of concubines the emperor kept, Yuan was particularly impressed with one who had "a pair of dragon eyes and a neck of a phoenix." Yuan secretly told his friend that this woman would become China's ruler one day, which turned out to be exactly the case. This concubine was none other than Wu Zetian (A.D. 625–684), who became emperor after the death of Li Shimin—the only female emperor in China's history.

Another story goes that when Fan Xuanling was an ordinary man, he and his friend Li Shensu went to see Yuan for a face reading. Li was a very arrogant man, thinking highly of himself and little of others. Much to his chagrin, Yuan pointed to Li and said: "You can best become a sixth rank official. It is very hard for you to climb to the fifth rank." Upon hearing this, Li was very much displeased, but said nothing for quite a while. Later he broke the silence and asked: "How about Mr. Fan?" Replied Yuan, "Alas, this gentleman is going to be the top official in the country. If you really want to become a fifth rank official, this is the person to ask." True to Yuan's predictions, Fan Xuanling later became a famous premier, and he asked the emperor to endow a fifth rank title to his friend Li Shensu. When Fan's petition was finally approved by the emperor, his friend Li had been dead for several months.

In terms of literature, perhaps the greatest influence on this metaphysical aspect of traditional Chinese culture is exerted by two names: Chen Xiyi and Yuan Liuzhuan. Chen Xiyi was nicknamed Ma Yi and lived during the Song Dynasty (A.D. 960–1279). Chen was born with a handsome face, but with strange bones in his forehead. When a Taoist immortal met him in the famous Hua Mountains, he was impressed with the greatness of Chen's appearance. The Taoist said to himself: "This man will become an immortal if not an emperor." The Taoist decided to teach Chen his secret knowledge of face reading. When Chen reached Luoyang in central China, he heard that Zhao Kuanyin had set up a new dynasty called Song. He gladly said to his friends:

"The world will be peaceful now." And he returned to the Hua mountains and became a recluse. Combining the teachings of his teacher with his own rich experience in face reading, Chen wrote the classic *Divine Physiognomy of Ma Yi*.

Divine Physiognomy of Ma Yi is by far the best known and most widely read Chinese book on the art of face reading; not because it is the earliest work in this field, but because it is the most comprehensive. Chen Xiyi elaborates on almost every facial feature of significance in describing and predicting fate. The book is well organized and easy to follow, even for those who have no previous knowledge of the subject. No wonder it has been the most popular book on physiognomy in China. Most significantly, it is in this book that a timing dimension was first added to a human face. It tells us where in the face to look for information regarding specific years in our lives. This is little short of a road map in face reading, which makes face reading a systematic art. However, the book does not pay enough attention to the differences between a male face and a female face. This was most likely due to the fact that traditional Chinese culture was completely male-centered. When the book was written, females were considered affiliates and attached to the male. The illustrations in it are quite rough and too vague to be really helpful to the reader. I think this is because Chen did not put

much effort in learning how to draw human faces. Given his isolated and highly independent personality, it was too much for him to ask for help.

Not long afterwards, Yuan Liuzhuan of the Ming dynasty (A.D. 1368–1644) wrote his own classic *Divine Physiognomy of Liuzhuan*, which was the first to largely focus on the description of women and children. This makes up for the deficiencies in Chen's book. This is another well organized and widely read book on physiognomy. Its major contribution to the theory and practice of face reading lies in the clear demarcation it has drawn between a male and a female face. Mainly through this book we have come to know that although we are all humans and share exactly the same facial features, our individual gender does make a difference—sometimes a vital difference—in the interpretation of some of the facial features. Another major contribution of this book is its detailed discussion of children's faces, which are more difficult to read and diagnose, if only because they are bound to have many changes during the course of their lives. Some later works have made modifications to Yuan's book, and incorporate its contents into theirs.

The prestige and popularity enjoyed by the art of face reading can also be seen in the fact that many Chinese officials were themselves serious practitioners of physiognomy, and were proud to display their skills in this respect. The great scholarly general Zen Guofan of the Qing Dynasty (A.D. 1644–1911) is one example. Zen's name is a buzzword in China because of his extraordinary literary achievements and, more importantly, because of his successful suppression of the Taiping Rebellion in the mid-eighteenth century. This rebellion ran rampant for ten years and spread over more than half of China's territory. However, not everybody knows that Zen Guofan was also a great face reader. The story goes that one day his student Li Hongzhang, who later became prime minister in the late Qing Dynasty, invited him to make a trip to the camp to help Li with his strategic personnel decisions. Zen looked briefly at Li's subordinates and came up with accurate descriptions and predictions of the personalities and fortunes of Li's major subordinates.

In his book, *Bing Jian*, Zen summarized the art of face reading based on his long experience with personnel. It is said that he based his decisions regarding hiring, promoting, and dismissing largely on the basis of physiognomy. He admitted that he owed a good part of his military success to his mastery of the art of face reading. It was face reading that enabled him to choose the best of soldiers among a vast sea of people, and put them in positions appropriate to their respective ability and personality, so that everybody could utilize their talents to the best.

Another famous dignitary in the Chin Dynasty who spent a lot of time studying face reading was Tao Shu, a governor-general of Hunan and Hubei provinces. Tao went a step further in his application of face divination, bringing it to bear on the choice of marriage partners. With his rare foresight and sagacity, he hand-picked Hu Linyi as his son-in-law while Hu still a poor playboy. Tao's subordinates all laughed at his "foolish" choice, and often told him about misconduct on the part of his son-in-law. Tao typically responded with a smile, saying, "Let [Hu] play for a while as he likes. Next year he will be too busy to behave like this any more." The Taiping Rebellion broke out the following year and Hu was summoned by the emperor to command an army against the rebels. He did such a wonderful job in suppressing the rebellion that two years later the emperor promoted him to the position of governor-general.

Tao Shu also proposed the marriage between his only son and the daughter of Zuo Zhongtang, while Zuo was still a lowly primary school teacher in the countryside of Hunan province. Tao did this when he first met Zuo Zhongtang during his inspection tour of the countryside. As Zuo humbly declined the offer, saying that this would not be a good match due to the wide gap between their families in wealth and social position, Tao dismissed the idea and encouraged Zuo: "Don't worry about that. Your future will be much brighter than mine." As if to live up to Tao's expectations and absolute confidence in him, Zuo Zhongtang rose rapidly to power during the Taiping Rebellion, and eventually became a premier. Indeed, Zuo is regarded by many as one of the greatest generals and statesmen in the history of China.

Modern examples of face reading can be found in dignitaries such as Chiang Kai-shek. Chiang is said to have employed the art of face divination to aid in strategic personnel decisions. I am told that at the eve of the major military showdown between Mao and Chiang in 1948, also known as the "Huai Hai Campaign" during China's civil war, Chiang Kai-shek spent many a sleepless night trying to fill the position of commander-in-chief for his army. He was expecting a showdown with Mao's army headed by Deng Xiaoping. Eventually he came up with the name of Liu Zhi, a well-known mediocre general. This strategic decision on the part of Chiang surprised everyone. When questioned about the rationale behind Liu's appointment, Chiang told his close subordinates that Liu had a very auspicious face (with which I agree). Apparently, Chiang drew heavily on the art of face reading to come up with this key personnel decision. He hoped that the individual good luck on the part of his key generals would help determine the outcome of the war and bring good luck to his regime.

Unfortunately, Chiang was only partly right. The outcome of the Huai Hai campaign turned out to be the "Waterloo" for Chiang's army. From then on, his regime began an all-out defense and rapid collapse. History, however, did back up Chiang's decision. Liu Zhi, Chiang's surprise choice for commander-in-chief, was the only one of the six top generals on the Nationalist side directing the campaign who safely returned. The other five were either killed in action, committed suicide, or were captured. Without a doubt, there were some connections between the personal fates of the key commanders and the outcome of the war, but this should not be stretched too far. After all, they are really two different things. For a military campaign with the magnitude of the Huai Hai Campaign, which very much determined the fate of Chiang's regime, it would have been better to have related Chiang's own fate, rather than that of his generals, with the outcome of the war.

The practice of face reading has been banned in China for about four decades since the defeat and the ensuing fllight of Chiang Kai-shek and his followers to the island of Taiwan in 1949. Mao Tse-tung banned it under the allegation of "feudal superstition," although in private life, Mao himself was a firm believer in the art. However, it has staged a brisk comeback since 1990. It is largely studied by intellectuals, and also cadres, and is widely practiced on street corners in major cities. People from all walks of life, including high-ranking party officials and army generals, show their interest in the art, although often "underground." Police officers do interfere with the practice every now and then. They sometimes disperse the crowds of clients in the street and sometimes take over the money made by the face readers; but they just cannot stop it. It seems to grow more and more popular with each passing day.

One evidence of its popularity is this: to satisfy employees' curiosity and need of face reading, some companies in China these days hire face readers to provide physiognomic services to their employees as part of their year-end bonus. The government just turns a half-closed eye to the practice of face reading. One Shanghai-based face reader in particular has been enjoying excellent business for many years, ever since he accurately predicted Jiang Zeming's coming to power as China's president in the wake of the gov-

ernment crackdown on the student movement in Tiananmen Square in 1989.

While dramatic changes have taken place since face reading made its debut in the ancient soil of China, the fundamental principles underlying face reading remain unchanged. However, significant modifications need to be made for analyzing a female face. Obviously, women are no longer mere dependents of their husbands and children. Equal education and, in particular, the women's liberation movement have created unprecedented opportunities for women. Nowadays, hardly anything that can be accomplished by men is beyond the reach and capability of women.

Without a doubt, the fascinating art of face reading will continue to play a significant role in the political, social, cultural, and personal events in China for a long, long time to come. I also think it has a promising future in the personnel and strategic decision-making processes of both private corporations and government agencies throughout the world.

Chapter 2

Principles of Chinese Face Reading

Face reading is an extremely old art. Consequently, many people think that it is derived from the I Ching, the earliest book on Chinese divination, and possibly the oldest book in the world. The I Ching, or "Book of Changes," played a major role in the development of Chinese philosophical thinking, and is just as important today as it ever has been. However, it has played only a minor role in the development of face reading. The I Ching taught that the universe is in a process of constant change and, by understanding the timing and nature of these changes, we can take advantage of them.

Everything in the world is subject to change. Not even our faces can escape this rule. This is proven in the changes our faces undergo as we age. To a student of face divination, such changes indicate a turn in the tide of fortune. Besides such natural causes of change, our moral status and behavior can also trigger facial changes. In the parlance of Chinese physiognomy, one's face changes with one's mind. In other words, good deeds and intentions bring about positive changes in fate as reflected in the face, while bad deeds and malicious intentions cause unfortunate changes. This principle of physiognomy is encouraging to those who were not born with good fate or a good face. Even those who are endowed with a good face should keep these words in mind, for nothing is constant, least of all good luck.

There are seven basic principles that need to be understood before we can determine what makes a face good or bad.

The Principle of System

The human face is a system in itself; a system of life information, if you will. As such, individual features are related to each other and should not be taken in isolation. Each feature is a building block of the face and should be studied carefully on an individual basis. These separate interpretations must then be combined to arrive at correct and comprehensive conclusions about one's fate. Indeed, it is in this systematic analysis of the entire face that the secrets of fate are revealed.

The Principle of Yin and Yang

The ancient Chinese tended to view things in the universe in terms of yin and yang, which can be roughly regarded as two polar opposites. Broadly speaking, yin is the principle realized on earth, while yang is the principle realized in heaven. This pair of polarities stands for almost everything in the universe. Individually, each polarity commands a bizarre constellation of objects, properties, and phenomena. Yin stands for the earth, the female, the moon, the night, benevolence, darkness, softness, water, etc. Yang represents the heaven, the male, the sun, the day, righteousness, brightness, hardness, fire, etc. Indeed, such a list of opposites can run the length of a book. It is in the combination, interrelation, and interdependence of these two polarities that everything in the universe has, and will, come into being, including humans.

It is stated in the I Ching that yin standing alone will not yield, just as yang standing alone will not grow. From this statement evolves a Chinese divination rule known as "left for the male and right for the female." This rule holds in both Chinese physiognomy and Chinese palmistry. In palmistry, when reading a person's hand, it is the left hand that counts for a male, whereas it is the right hand that counts for a female.

In exactly the same manner, Chinese face divination holds that all facial loca-

men →
symmetrical
women ←

Principles of Chinese Face Reading — 11

tions and features that are symmetrical, such as the ears, eyes, eyebrows, and cheekbones, should be analyzed from the left side first if the person being read is a man, but from the right side if the person is a female. The same goes for age counting or mapping. Every age from one to ninety corresponds with a certain location on the face. For example, ages one through seven are located on the ear: for a male, they are on left ear; for a female, they are on the right ear. (See chapter 5 for more on age mapping.)

This principle and others create a strict line of demarcation between the male and female. This is based on traditional Chinese culture in which the emphasis has always been on the male. That is how the observations and interpretations in Chinese face reading have been written. For some not very good historical reasons, women in traditional China were considered appendages of their husbands, if they were lucky enough to even have a husband. They did not assume an independent personality, and were strongly discouraged, if not prohibited, from doing so. While I have attempted to present more modern interpretations, the way the woman's face is presented in this book is based on the traditional interpretations of Chinese face reading, and should be put in that context.

Definitely, times have changed. Some of the interpretations of fate given may sound stereotypical and even offensive to today's

modern woman. Women in China and around the world have acquired more equality with men and are no longer considered inferior to their male counterparts. This change in social values warrants a new set of physiognomical rules to be laid down for the reading of female faces, but that would be the task of another book. While there are still some areas where the yin and yang principle still apply, interpretations for many of the facial features can be equally applied to both men and women to get a more modern reading.

The Principle of the Five Elements

The principle of the five elements is as important to the theory and practice of face divination as it is to many other aspects of traditional Chinese culture, such as acupuncture, medicine, astrology, and feng shui. Indeed, it is one of the guiding principles of all philosophical thinking in China. As face divination attempts to reveal the secret relationships between man and the universe, it is logical to assume that many secrets can be discovered by studying the interactions of the five elements from which the universe and human beings were born.

The ancient Chinese believed that the universe and everything in it were composed of five basic elements: wood, fire, water, metal, and earth. They also thought that man's fate was a combination of these elements. The relationships between these five elements are at once mutually productive and mutually destructive. (See Figure 2.1.) In terms of mutual production, for instance, water nourishes wood, wood feeds fire, fire produces earth, earth creates metal, and metal yields water, completing a cycle of mutual production. At the same time, there is a completely different type of relationship working among these elements, one of mutual destruction. Therefore, water quenches fire, fire melts metal, metal cuts wood, wood dredges earth, and earth stops water, thus completing the cycle of mutual destruction. It is this dual relationship among the five basic elements that keeps the universe functioning and in balance.

Of the five elements, water is the most flexible, with properties of soaking and descending to lower elevations; fire is the most violent, which burns and moves upward; wood is straightforward and long in nature; metal is conceived to be sharp and square in nature; and earth provides the working ground for all the other elements and is therefore thick and stable.

By using their strong imaginations and sharp insight, the ancient Chinese set up a long list of correspondences between the five elements and natural objects and social phenomena. These include, but are not limited to, tastes, smells, musical notes, seasons of the year, colors, human organs, and ethi-

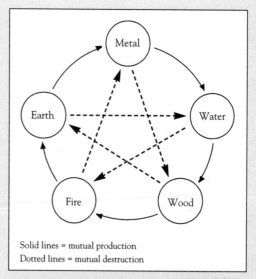

Solid lines = mutual production
Dotted lines = mutual destruction

Figure 2.1: Mutual production and mutual destruction of the five elements

cal values. Table 2.1 on page 13 provides a shortened list of these correspondences.

These five elements may be used to classify any phenomenon in nature and human society. For instance, traditional Chinese medicine uses the five elements to explain the interrelations and interactions of different organs of the body, to show how a deficit or excess in one organ can disturb the balance among all organs and lead to illness.

From a face reading viewpoint, each of the five elements also stands for a particular facial feature, complexion, and shape. For instance, the element earth represents the nose, water the mouth, fire the forehead,

Element	Direction	Features	Color	Season
Fire	South	Forehead	Red	Summer
Metal	West	Eye	White	Autumn
Wood	East	Ears	Green	Spring
Water	North	Mouth	Black	Winter
Earth	Center	Nose	Yellow	Mid-season
Element	**Shape**	**Value**	**Organ**	
Fire	Pointed	Propriety	Heart	
Metal	Square	Righteousness	Lung	
Wood	Long	Kindness	Liver	
Water	Round	Intelligence	Kidney	
Earth	Thick	Reliability	Spleen	

Table 2.1: Five elements and their correspondences

metal the eyes, and wood the ears. For face shapes, a square face belongs to metal, a round one to water, a long face to wood, and so on. (For more on face shapes see chapter 6.) Each face must be individually evaluated on the basis of the five elements before accurate conclusions can be drawn.

The ideal situation in face reading with regard to the five elements is one in which balance and harmony prevail. This is achieved, of course, through mutual com-plementation among the elements. The Chinese fathers of face divination hold that a face with all the features in balance and harmony with one another is an auspicious sign, while a face with features that are out of balance with one another is an inauspi-cious sign, i.e., bad luck. Balance in the shape, size, length, and color of facial features means balance in the five elements and thus, good fate. So a small face with a large nose is generally not considered a well-balanced face. In fact, it is usually an unfavorable sign indicating a violent, miserable death.

The Principle of Harmony and Balance

Chinese physiognomy and Confucian philosophy all stress the importance of balance and harmony in nature and human activities. Balance and harmony refer to the golden rule of having "just enough" of everything—neither an excess nor deficit, neither too much nor too little. To have too much of something is considered as bad as having too little. This is as true of nature as it is of human society. Natural calamities such as volcanoes and earthquakes, and man-made disasters such as social unrest and revolution, all result from violating this golden rule of harmony and balance.

Confucius formally theorized this concept into a fundamental principle of Confucianism known as the Doctrine of the Middle Way. According to Confucius, people should stick to the "middle way" in everything they do and feel, avoiding the extremes. To apply the Doctrine of the Middle Way to our individual lives is to avoid misfortune and regret, and to enjoy peace of mind, harmonious relationships, and good health. It is little wonder that such an important and universal a principle as the middle way has been embraced and taken seriously by face readers.

The Confucian principle of harmony is heavily utilized in face reading, although Confucius himself was not a face reader. Masters of face divination hold that facial features in harmony with or complementary to each other are a sign of prosperity. In light of this principle, some features that are unfavorable when taken alone can be considered favorable because they are in harmony with the other features. For example, a long nose is normally considered a favorable feature, but if it is set in a short face, it becomes unfavorable because it is out of harmony with the rest of the face.

The Principle of Man-Animal Resemblance

An interesting and important feature of Chinese face reading lies in the relationship between animals and human beings. Traditional Chinese philosophy holds that since animals and humans were created by the same Way, or the Grand Law of Nature, it is only natural that both would have something in common if they resemble one another. This idea is clearly elucidated by Gui Gu-Tze who said: "Originally, man had no form; he just assumed the shape from nature. Thus, some of them adopted the form of birds while others took the shape of animals." Animal traits are often used as reference points for reading human faces; if a person has a resemblance to one kind of animal, that person will assume certain characteristics of that animal. For example, a tiger is considered bold and aggressive. If someone looks very similar to a tiger, that person would then be considered bold and aggressive as well.

Resemblance to certain animals can also reveal how lucky you will be in your career and if you will hold a high position in government or business. See appendix A for a complete explanation of man-animal resemblance along with a list of of types.

Another interesting fact about this principle is that Chinese face divination borrows legendary animals and birds, such as the dragon, phoenix, and unicorn. Contrary to the Western tradition in which the dragon is considered a fierce, evil animal, in China, the dragon is the most noble animal, symbolizing supreme authority, power, strength, and luck. Similarly, the phoenix is an imperial emblem—the female counterpart of the dragon. The unicorn is yet another lucky animal, with the body of a horse and the head of a dragon.

As such, it sometimes takes imagination in addition to a knowledge of zoology to apply this principle.

The Principle of Implicitness

The art of Chinese face reading goes beyond the study of facial features. A master face reader will also look at other characteristics of the person being read, such as their hands, feet, the sound of their voices, their eating manners, even how they walk or sleep. Since these characteristics are beyond the face itself, they are considered implicit from the viewpoint of face reading, although they still bear significantly on one's fate as a whole. All too often, these non-facial features are neglected and ignored by face reading neophytes. This is one reason why they often arrive at wrong or inaccurate conclusions about a person. However, these implicit, non-facial features cannot escape the sharp eyes and alert ears of an experienced master face reader.

To show the significant relationship of these implicit features to the explicit facial ones, here are some historical observations. Chinese historical records tell us that the Beginning Emperor of the Chin Dynasty was a cruel dictator who buried alive more than 400 intellectuals and burned all the useful books except those on medicine and agriculture. He feared that knowledge and people with knowledge would rebel against his totalitarian rule and eventually topple his dictatorship. The interesting thing from the viewpoint of face reading is that this emperor had some strange features and characteristics, one of which was that his voice sounded like that of a wolf. Face reading masters interpreted this as an indication of extreme cruelty.

Emperor Liu Bei (160–223), and Emperor Wu of the Jin Dynasty (265–420) each had a pair of hands that could reach their knees when they stood straight. So also did Emperor Tai Zhu of the Late Zhou Dynasty (951–960). Face reading masters took this to indicate supreme national authority.

Yuan Tiangang was not only excellent in reading explicit features, but he also had a special eye for, and understanding of, implicit features as well. One of his contemporaries, named Li Qiao, had three brothers who had already died—all before the age of thirty. Li was twenty. Li's mother was therefore very worried about her only remaining son. Knowing that Yuan Tiangang was an expert on face reading, she invited Yuan to her house. As soon as he caught sight of Li, Yuan told his mother: "This son of yours will also die before thirty."

This devastated the woman. "Look, sir, how strong my son is," she pleaded. "Would you please spend some more time with my son to better understand him?" Yuan agreed and slept in the same room with Li Qiao. In the early hours of the morning, Yuan woke up and put his finger close to Li's nostrils. He could detect no breathing, but Li's heart was still beating. Then Yuan put his fingers close to Li's ears, and was surprised to find that the boy breathed through his ears! This was known as "tortoise breathing," a very auspicious sign. The next morning, Yuan congratulated Li's mother: "Your son will not only survive the age of thirty, he will become a top official in the country."

Many years later, Li was made a premier to China's only female emperor, Wu Zetian, and lived to be more than sixty years old.

Perhaps it is not an overstatement to say that Chinese face reading has left no stone unturned in its effort to reveal the secrets of fate by means of facial and body features. For example, Wu Zetian and Empress Lu, the first wife of Liu Bang, both had extremely long pubic hair, which is said to have reached their knees when stretched. This feature was viewed as both an indication of high political authority and extreme eroticism. Although this is an interesting observation in Chinese body divination, it is hard to verify and goes beyond the scope of face reading.

The Principle of Geographic Location

Chinese physiognomy holds that people from certain areas of the country take with them, or are supposed to take with them, certain features characteristic of that area. Different parts of the face have been assigned different geographic orientations. Thus, the forehead stands for the south, the chin for the north, the nose for the central area, and so on. This goes back to the five elements and the correspondence chart (Table 2.1, page 13) where the forehead corresponds with the element of fire, which corresponds with the direction of south.

The same goes for the chin, where it corresponds with the the element of water, which corresponds with the direction of north, and so on.

Geographic differences affect certain characteristics of the facial features, too. For instance, it has been observed that those from the northern part of China usually have shorter foreheads but longer chins than those from the southern part of the country. On the other hand, Southerners in China are supposed to have higher, broader foreheads and lighter eyebrows than their northern neighbors. All this means that the forehead carries greater weight for Southerners and the chin carries greater weight for Northerners.

However, there are always exceptions to the rule. The guiding principle in this regard is that if a Northerner looks like a South-erner, it is an auspicious sign, and vice versa. For instance, Kublai Khan (1214–1294), the founding father of the Yuan Dynasty, was born with a face like a Southerner—a high, broad, and sanguine forehead in the shape of a slightly convex mirror, a pair of delicate and handsome eyebrows, and medium stature—although he was from the northern part of the country in Mongolia. By contrast, Mao's appearance was highly suggestive of a Northerner, although he was born in the southern province of Hunan: tall and big of stature, a big head and broad face, a pair of outstanding cheekbones plus a large, square chin.

This principle applies equally well to people who are not from China. Adjustments will need to be made to the particular ethnic group and its cultural norms.

永美命

Chapter 3

Structure of the Face: A Macro Perspective

The human face contains a world of secrets. It harbors a wealth of valuable information about both the person and those closely related to that person. Since time immemorial, the Chinese have shown a keen interest in revealing and obtaining the secrets and information hidden in the face. They have studied it at different ages, from different perspectives, and from different approaches.

One of the perspectives they have taken is a broad one—a macro perspective. This approach takes a quick look at the face in order to get an overall view. The beauty of the macro perspective lies in its efficiency. In a short period of time, one can get a broad idea of a person's fate.

A macro perspective reveals which of the three stages of life the person is in: childhood, young adult, middle age, or old age. It can also reveal approximately how much a person can achieve in this lifetime, what kind of profession would suit the person best, and the overall well-being of the person in terms of finances, family, relationships, marriage, career, and promotion, etc. It is not the purpose of this approach to obtain a detailed account of all the information contained in a face, from year to year. That is the purpose of a micro analysis, which takes into account each minute portion of a face and each individual facial feature. We leave that task to a later chapter.

The theoretical basis of this macro approach is contained in three key concepts, or subsystems, of Chinese face reading. They are the Three Portions, the Five Mountains, and the Twelve Palaces. While these concepts are separate in theory, they are intrinsically interconnected. In fact, they often overlap into each other's territory. That is to say, the same face, or the same facial feature, can be viewed and described from different perspectives.

Let's explore these three subsystems one by one.

Three Portions

Most people look at someone's face and get a general impression of it in terms of shape, size, color, attractiveness, and so on. In fact, that is all an outsider can tell about a face. Most people have no idea what the different shapes, sizes, and colors mean in terms of human fate, even if the face is their own.

This is not the case for a master face reader. Typically, when a face reader encounters a face, he will instinctively measure it by first dividing it into three sections using the Three Portions concept: the upper portion, the middle portion, and the lower portion. (See Figure 3.1, page 21.)

The upper portion of a face runs from the hairline to the eyebrows. Basically, it occupies the entire area of forehead. The middle portion picks up where the upper portion leaves off, moving downward to the nose tip. Everything that is below the tip of the nose is then considered the lower portion of the face.

There is an alternative naming system for the three portions based on a traditional Chinese concept: the upper portion corresponds to heaven, the middle portion to man, and the lower portion to earth. This is the concept of the heaven-man-earth trinity, a vital one in traditional Chinese culture and philosophical thinking. It is so deeply rooted in the traditional Chinese way of thinking that it has been applied to almost every subject of significant importance, including health care and feng shui.

The Three Portions system is an important yet convenient starting point in the

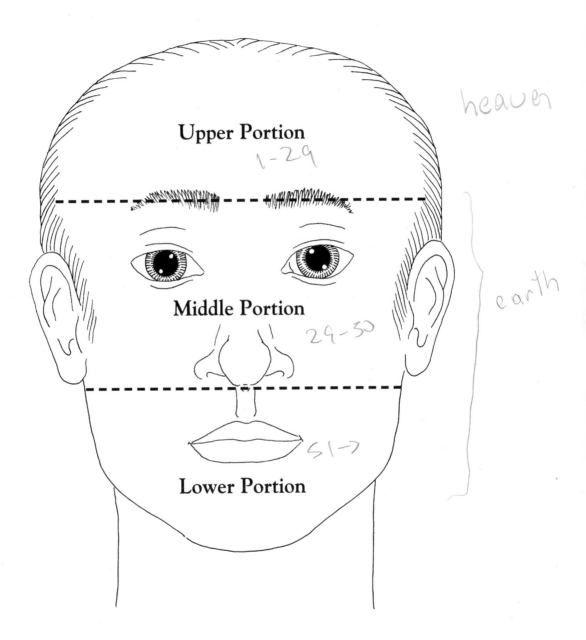

Figure 3.1: Three Portions system

art of face divination. A great deal of valuable information can be found by measuring the size, length, and relative proportions of the three areas, as well as by assessing their harmony and balance.

These three portions of the face also correspond to the three stages of life. The upper portion corresponds to one's childhood period (between the ages of one and twenty-eight); the middle portion corresponds to middle age (between twenty-nine and fifty); and the lower portion corresponds to old age—the sunset period of life (between fifty-one and seventy-five). It is important to keep in mind that these definitions of life periods are purely age-oriented; they have nothing to do with the quality of life in terms of health, career, relationships, or wealth.

You may notice that old age is only counted to seventy-five when today, many people live past that age. This is because the Chinese ancients held that most people would not live over the age of seventy-five. The next chapter will discuss this age factor in more detail.

This classification of a face into three portions and their correspondence with the three periods in life, along with their relative size or proportion, gives a face reader some readily available information about what is or will be the best and/or worst period in someone's life. For instance, if the upper portion of your face is broader and

longer than the other two portions, it is an indication that you should have had a happy childhood, most likely because you were born into a happy family where your parents either had good careers or inherited some fortune from their parents.

Similarly, if the middle portion of your face is the best one and is much longer than the upper portion, you benefit little from your family background but have achieved or will achieve considerable success in middle age, through your own efforts or with the help of friends, a spouse, or employers. Middle age is the time most people enter society, build a career, and set up a family. This is the period in life when the combination of knowledge and energy is at its best. Therefore, it holds the greatest promise for most people. It is little wonder that most historical figures in all fields of human endeavor make their marks on history in their middle age.

If the lower portion is the best part of your face, you will have a relatively happy old age.

It is important to keep in mind that the three portions of a face are separate indicators of fate in different stages of life. Each of the portions stands alone, although they are connected and continuous. Just as wealth does not guarantee health, a happy childhood is not necessarily followed by a miserable middle age, nor does a happy middle age necessarily lead to a happy old age.

Each stage of life has to be weighed and evaluated on its own basis. In other words, we have only to look at the forehead and eyebrows to judge a person's fate in the early stage of life; at a person's eyes and nose to find out information regarding the person's fate in middle age; and the mouth and chin to know how the person is or will be doing in old age.

What, then, makes a good portion or a bad portion? Roughly speaking, a good upper portion is a forehead that is broad, high, light, smooth, and slightly protruding, paired with orderly eyebrows. By contrast, a bad upper portion is a narrow, low, and dim forehead full of wrinkles, plus a pair of chaotic eyebrows. (All of these facial features and terms are discussed in greater detail in their individual chapters.)

A good middle portion is comprised of a pair of bright, penetrating eyes and a straight, long, high, and fleshy nose. A bad middle portion has a pair of dim, unfocused eyes and a low, broken, skinny, crooked, or pointed nose.

A good lower portion consists of a good mouth and a broad, thick, and long chin, while a bad lower portion has an inauspicious mouth and a short, narrow, and pointed chin.

With regard to the length or proportion of the three portions, we find the principle of balance and harmony asserting itself. This rule of face divination says that the ideal case would have the three portions of the face all roughly the same length, producing a sense of harmony and balance. One who possesses such a face will have a smooth and prosperous career and family life, and will never have to worry about his or her livelihood.

If the face portions are not balanced, one would rather have a better middle portion than upper portion. This is because too smooth a childhood often spoils a child, leaving one ill prepared for a tough, competitive middle life. (For this reason, many Chinese actually consider a prosperous childhood a great misfortune.)

If a good middle portion is followed by a sharply receding lower portion, one's brilliant career will have an abrupt, violent ending, for a poor lower portion indicates a miserable old age. This is exactly the case with Lin Biao and Liu Shaoqi, the would-be successors to Mao, hand-picked by Mao himself. They were cruelly killed by their common protégé when they were in their sixties and seventies, respectively.

Five Mountains

In this system, five features of the face are assigned to five of the most famous mountains in China: the forehead is likened to the Mountains Heng in the south; the nose is likened to the Mountains Song in central China; the chin stands for the Mountains

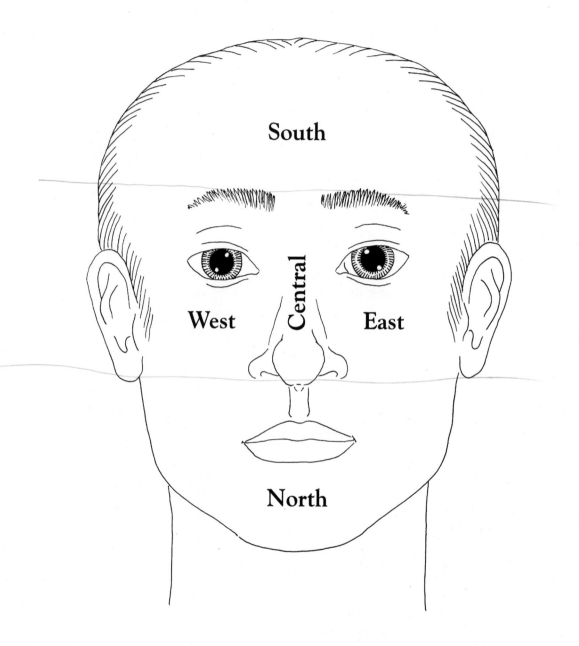

Figure 3.2: Five Mountains system

Hen in the north; the left cheekbone, the Mountains Tai in the east; and the right cheekbone, the Mountains Hua in the west. (See Figure 3.2, page 24.)

These five mountains are reputed for their height and magnificence so, therefore, one should have all five facial features standing out prominently. If this is the case, one will have great fortune, a happy family, an outstanding career, and hold a high social position in life. On the other hand, if any of the features are not very prominent or sunken, or have been injured, the luck of the person is weakened, and will most likely result in misfortune or even calamity in time.

Another significance of this system is that different weights should be given to these five facial features depending on the geographic location where a person is born (principle of geographic location). For instance, since the forehead is associated with the most famous mountain in southern China, the forehead should then be given greater weight than the other features when reading the face of someone from southern China. Similarly, the nose is of special importance to people born in the central part of the country, while for those born in northern China, the chin is of the greatest importance.

This principle applies to all ethnic groups in the world, so long as the country in which a specific ethnic group resides can be geographically classified into southern, northern, eastern, and western parts.

The Twelve Palaces

For another macro perspective of the face, the fathers of Chinese face divination have identified Twelve Palaces, often used as a face reading shortcut. The Twelve Palaces system is an extensive one and is discussed fully in the next chapter.

永美命

Chapter 4

The Twelve Palaces

The Twelve Palaces system is another way of obtaining a broad summary of a person's fate. It is a useful system as the palaces are fairly easy to identify and are basically self-explanatory in connotation. Reading the Twelve Palaces is like a face reading shortcut when we only want a quick overview of someone's fate.

The exact reason why these facial locations are termed "palaces" is lost in the mists of history, but we can guess that the Chinese fathers thought highly of every part of the face because they are symbolic of our fate. The system of the Twelve Palaces is meant to be a complement, rather than an alternative, to the systems of the Three Portions and Five Mountains discussed in chapter 3. Together they provide a clear picture of a person's fate in the macro sense of the term. Therefore, it is highly advisable to combine these three subsystems in a macro approach towards a face.

The palaces are illustrated in Figure 4.1 on page 29. They are listed in order from the upper part to the lower part of the face, moving from left to right. In actual practice, however, one does not have to follow this order. Usually, a face reader can go directly to a specific palace of interest.

You may encounter some unfamiliar terms or descriptions of features, such as "bright," "yellow," or "dented." For more clarification, refer to the specific chapter for that feature being described. If it's a color that's unclear, refer to chapter 7, "Face Color and Spirit."

Career Palace

The Career Palace is situated at the very center of the forehead. As the name implies, this place symbolizes career success, social position, chances of promotion, and how high one can ascend in the corporate or government hierarchy.

An auspicious Career Palace is a forehead that is broad, smooth, rounded, and bright (light or illuminating). Such a Career Palace indicates a smooth and successful career, a high social position, and honor.

People with an auspicious Career Palace are usually ambitious and eloquent, with good leadership and communication skills. Indeed, it is these important qualities that drive them on to career success. It is also highly desirable, traditionally for males, that this palace contains a protruding bone. (See chapter 20 on bones for more information.)

If the Career Palace is dented, sunken, narrow, or dark (darker color than the rest of the face), it is an inauspicious sign indicating frustration and failure in one's career, poor communication skills, and a lack of drive and competitiveness.

Parent Palaces

The Parent Palaces are located high on the sides (angles) of the forehead. They indicate the health of one's parents, the relationship between the parents, as well as the person's relationship with them.

If these areas are bright, shiny, broad, and fleshy, your parents will enjoy good health and longevity. Your parents love each other and you have a loving relationship with your parents. You can also expect significant financial and political help from your parents.

However, if these areas are narrow, covered by hair, sunken, or marred by lines (wrinkles) and moles, you have inauspicious Parent Palaces. Among other things, this indicates that at least one of your parents

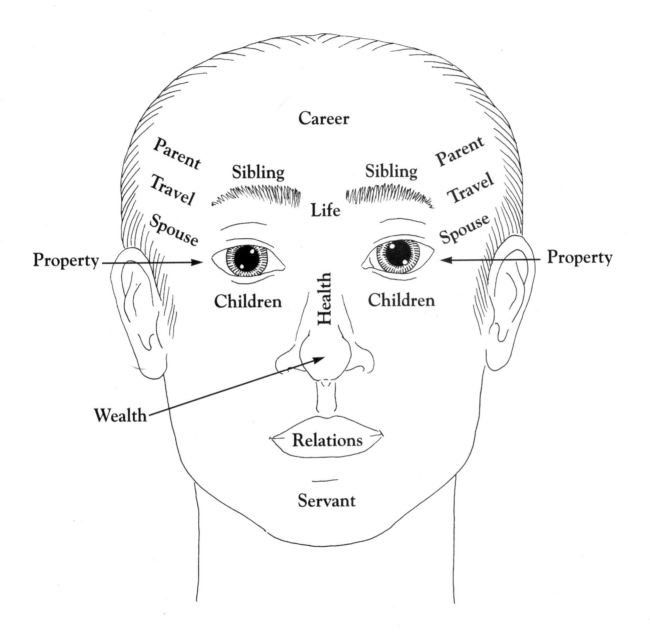

Figure 4.1: The Twelve Palaces

will die early. Even if they both live long lives, they may be separated or divorced, and possibly not even be on speaking terms. Your relationship with your parents will also not be good, and you cannot expect much help from them.

Life Palace

The technical term for the location of the Life Palace is the glabella, or the space between the eyebrows. In Chinese physiognomy it is known as "Yintang," or literally, the "Hall of Seal." Again as the name implies, this is an extremely important palace that bears directly on life itself. It indicates one's energy, luck early in life, career, and help from others. Indeed, it can be regarded as the spring of life energy. A good Life Palace ensures a good inherited health, a life that will most likely last past the age of thirty, a good family background, and a smooth career early in life.

In China, a child born with a good Life Palace is considered easy to raise, whereas one born with a poor Life Palace will cause the parents a lot of worry. The child may die at a young age, and even if he or she does survive childhood, there is a great chance that the child will have a difficult time passing the age of thirty. I have had the unpleasant experience of witnessing two of my childhood friends die before they were thirty. Both of them were highly intelligent and

talented; one excelled in mathematics, and the other was a poet. They had been regarded as geniuses at school, and both worked hard and studiously, with little time for nonsense. Unfortunately, their Life Palaces were narrow and dark, with the eyebrows almost joining—all negative signs in face reading. One died at the age of twenty-eight, and the other at twenty-nine. Coincidentally, both were killed in car accidents.

The Life Palace is judged by three dimensions: breadth, color, and topography. Chinese face reading holds that an auspicious Life Palace is broad, smooth, bright, shining, and yellow or rosy in color. In terms of breadth, this palace should be able to accommodate the width of two fingers. Generally speaking, the broader the Life Palace, the higher a social position one will hold, or the greater the power (material as well as mental) one will possess. I have seen people whose Life Palaces can accommodate three fingers. Of course, these are rare people who hold great promise for the future. Typically, a broad Life Palace indicates a smooth childhood, honor, and a leadership position.

On the other hand, if the space between the eyebrows is narrow, dark, dry, or dented, the person will have a hard childhood, and find it difficult to advance in a career or establish a family before the age of thirty. Frequently, this person lacks a good family background to fall on, and has to fight their own way in the world from an early age.

The color of the Life Palace has much to do with one's fortune or misfortune in the near future. This could be anywhere from one day to a month. Chinese physiognomy holds that the Life Palace should be bright, yellow or rosy, and shiny. This indicates a smooth life, free from disease, misfortune, or accidents. If the location is naturally rosy and shiny, one can expect some good tidings in the near future. This can be either marriage, promotion, financial gains, or a new baby. However, if the Life Palace is dull, dry, and dark, some misfortune can be expected. In such cases, masters of face reading will advise the person to be extremely cautious in speech and action, staying home when possible, avoiding driving, travel, gambling, and physical competition, and also praying often. Otherwise, some serious disease or misfortune is bound to overtake the person.

The third dimension to the reading of the Life Palace is topography. By topography I mean the "land form" of the area between the eyebrows. Is this area protruding, smooth, or depressed? As a physiognomical rule, smoothness is superior to depression, and protrusion is superior to smoothness.

A depressed Life Palace usually means financial, health, or legal troubles in early life. People with such a Life Palace may, for example, go bankrupt, suffer from a life-threatening disease, or spend some time in prison. Some of them may die before thirty for any of these reasons.

However, if the Life Palace is smooth, the transition from early age to middle age will be smooth, too. One is unlikely to have financial, health, or legal troubles during this transitional period in life. Better still, if this area protrudes, good inherited health and financial help are indicated.

Travel Palaces

The Travel Palaces are located at the temples, also called the solar areas. They indicate whether or not one will travel a lot in life, and whether one will have good luck during those travels.

In ancient China, clothing, food, shelter, and travel were considered the four basic necessities of life; hence, the importance of travel. No wonder, before they set out to travel, people would usually check their Travel Palaces to see if they should go ahead or stay at home.

Good Travel Palaces should be broad, bright, red or yellow, full and fleshy, unmarred by moles or lines, and uncovered by hair. These areas indicate material and/or spiritual gains from travel, plenty of enjoyable travel throughout life, and, more importantly in traditional Chinese society, a promising career promotion. People with good Travel Palaces will find professional success and romance in places far from their home towns. Of course, this does not mean that they cannot find success and marriage where they are born; it just means that they have more alternatives and choices, which is definitely a good thing, especially in modern times.

The reason why Travel Palaces indicate a career promotion lies in the fact that travel was a way of life for Chinese officials in the past. Chinese emperors did not want to see their officials rooted in one location, and therefore relocated them from time to time. Typically, for first-time appointments, the location was usually far away from home. In order to be an official and gain political position, one must be ready to travel. This was a basic requirement. Since more uncertainties and potential accidents can occur during travel than by staying at home, ambitious people naturally hoped that their upcoming official travel would be as smooth as their Travel Palaces.

Bad Travel Palaces are sunken, dark, or covered with moles or hair. Those with such Travel Palaces will have trouble and misfortune during travel, either by a loss of money, by sickness, or by an accident. There is usually not much fun in traveling for these people. Face readers will advise such people to think twice before they leave home on a long trip. If they have to go, as in the case of business, they are advised to carry with them some charms as protection against evil forces.

Sibling Palaces

The Sibling Palaces are located at the eyebrows. There lie the secrets about the quantity and quality of one's siblings and one's relationship with them.

If the eyebrows are long, graceful, and shiny, the person will have many brothers and sisters. All of them will be good, friendly, and helpful to each another, especially in money matters, since all of them will have successful careers.

On the other hand, if the eyebrows are haphazard, scattered, thin, mismatched, or short and broken, one will not have many siblings. The relationships among them are also bound to be difficult and cool, if not hostile. Most likely, people with such eyebrows will fight with their brothers and sisters over money and heritage. They will have more problems with each other than they will ever experience with acquaintances and are unable to count on each other for help.

Property Palaces

The Property Palaces are situated at the eyes. Here information is obtained about how much property one will own in life (property meaning a house, business, land investments, etc.).

Auspicious eyes signify, among other things, the ability to own property. As a general rule, if the eyes have large, black pupils and a penetrating gaze, the person will enjoy good luck in business and eventual ownership of real estate.

Inauspicious eyes mean the lack or loss of property. If the eyes are red and shy away from bright light, it is an indication of financial problems, which can be in the area of real estate.

Spouse Palaces

These palaces are located at the outside edges of the eyes, immediately below the temples. They are indications of the relationship between the spouses (and same-sex couples) and the quality of family life. Since marriage is an extremely important component in the quality of life, face divination attaches great weight to these locations.

Good Spouse Palaces are full, fleshy, rosy, bright, and smooth, with no moles on them. Such Spouse Palaces indicate a long-lasting, easy, and happy marriage.

If, however, these locations are dark, sunken, dented, full of lines, or marked with moles, the person has inauspicious Spouse Palaces. People with these Spouse Palaces have a hard time getting married. If they are married, they generally will not be happy.

Most likely, they will find that their spouses have ill health, a bad temperament, or die shortly after their marriage. Masters of face reading often advise such people to marry late in life, and with a considerable age gap between them so as to minimize the inauspicious effects of the bad Spouse Palaces.

Children Palaces

The small round areas right below the eyes are known as the Children Palaces. They indicate the quantity and quality of children one has, as well as one's relationship with them.

Auspicious Children Palaces are even, bright, smooth, and fleshy. This indicates that one will have many children who will be good, filial, and successful in their own careers, thus bringing honor to their parents.

If the Children Palaces are dark, dry, sunken, or marred by lines or moles, they indicate a lack of children or few children, who are subject to ill health, death, or mean-spiritedness. People with such palaces should not expect help and respect from their children. On the contrary, what they can expect from their children—if they have any—is trouble and sour relations.

Health Palace

The Health Palace is situated on the bridge of the nose, also called the dorsum. As the name indicates, it signifies one's health in life, especially in the early part of life, before the age of thirty.

An auspicious Health Palace means a nose bridge that is high, smooth, projected, and bright in color. Such a Health Palace indicates good health, a high level of energy, and courage.

Courage, oddly enough, does have a lot to do with one's health. This is because good health means that one possesses a strong reserve of qi energy in the body. According to the Chinese fathers, qi is the prime basis of life. Qi determines not only our health, but also our energy level, sexual vitality, work efficiency, and courage. People who are full of qi energy have a sanguine complexion, high work efficiency, better endurance, strong immunity, and great courage.

As with other elements essential to health, the qi level in the body normally declines with age as a matter of natural course. That is why, in general, the older one gets, the more timid one becomes. To attest to this truth, a Chinese proverb says: "Newborn calves are not afraid of tigers—young people are fearless." This subtle relationship between qi level and courage has been well explored by Chinese sages. Mencius, for one, was very proud of his ability to build up a strong qi reserve. On one occasion, when talking of a brave historical figure who dared to challenge even his

emperor, Mencius made this comment: "It is a rare thing that one is born with such strong qi. He should learn to treasure and preserve it throughout his life." This is exactly what Confucius accomplished, becoming an exception to the rule. Commenting on himself as an elderly man, he proudly declared: "Wealth cannot corrupt me; poverty cannot transform me; force cannot bend me." What great moral courage he had at that age—a marvelous reserve of qi energy.

An inauspicious Health Palace is indicated by a nose bridge that is crooked, lined, or dark in color. It indicates poor health, especially chronic diseases, and a low level of qi energy.

It should be noted that good health mentioned in this context refers mainly to whether or not one has a strong physical make-up. It does not necessarily mean disease. After all, health is a matter over which we ourselves have the greatest control. In other words, even if one is born with a weak physique or poor health or, in the parlance of Chinese health care, with insufficient qi energy, one still can manage to live a long and healthy life if one practices a healthy way of life on a daily basis.

People who are born with an auspicious Health Palace, have to work only half as hard to stay healthy. However, those who are born with an inauspicious Health Palace have to double their efforts and be more careful in order to enjoy health and longevity. Of course, this can be a fortune in disguise, depending on what you know and how you handle life. In fact, many people who live long lives are found to have a weak Health Palace. It is their willpower to be healthy and live a long life that eventually prevails. On the other hand, many people with an auspicious Health Palace have died young, because their strong physique makes them oblivious of the constant need to take care of their own health.

Wealth Palace

The Wealth Palace is composed of the nose tip and alar grooves ("wings" of the nose); basically the entire lower part of the nose. It signifies exactly what it says—one's ability to make money and to accumulate wealth.

A full, large, round, fleshy nose tip with fleshy, full wings and nostrils that are not easily visible is considered an excellent Wealth Palace. It ensures that one will have more than enough money to spend throughout one's life.

Indeed, one can become very rich with such a nose. While the nose tip is regarded as the wealth creator, the nose wings are considered treasures in Chinese face reading. Their function is to ensure that money earned is well kept. A person can be very capable of making money, but he or she may be very bad in managing and maintaining it. For this person, it is easy come, easy go, and in the end, the person does not have much set aside. Remember: It is not how much one earns, but how much one saves, that makes one rich.

If the nose tip is small, pointed, crooked, with large nostrils and contracted wings, it is considered an inauspicious Wealth Palace. People with such a Wealth Palace experience serious financial problems. Oftentimes, they will find it hard to make ends meet. Even if they possess great fortune at some point, they will most likely lose it, sooner or later. Since marital success and family happiness in today's world can depend so much on financial health, a bad Wealth Palace may also forebode an unhappy marriage and a troubled relationship.

Relations Palace

The Relations Palace falls on the mouth. In other words, one's mouth contains the information regarding one's relationships with others. In modern terms, it reveals one's interpersonal skills.

The fathers of face divination tell us that if the mouth is rosy, with thick and well-shaped lips, it is an indication of strong sexual vitality and good relationships with friends.

If the mouth is slanted, uneven, protruded, or dark in color, it indicates poor relationships within and outside of the family. Such people easily lend themselves to misunderstandings, either by their actions or words. They often offend others unintentionally, and do not have many friends. Others find them too peevish, selfish, and provocative to get along with. Therefore, fathers of face divination advise those with a poor Relations Palace to guard their mouth and think twice before they speak.

Servant Palace

The Servant Palace is located on the chin. The term "servant palace" relates to China's feudal age when the number of servants one possessed represented to a large extent the wealth and social position one held, since servants were considered personal property. While those days are gone, the term remains in face reading because it has gained a new meaning—power and authority. Today, the Servant Palace signifies the number of people under one's leadership or supervision. Of course, the more people you supervise or govern, the greater your power and the higher your position and honor.

A good Servant Palace is represented by a round, fleshy, long and protruding chin, while a bad Servant Palace is one that is narrow, short, thin, pointed, or depressed.

Chapter 5

Structure of the Face: A Micro Perspective

While a macrocosmic view of the face can give a general idea about the owner of the face in terms of broad timing, it does not tell the exact timing in which special events have happened or will happen. After all, fate is a matter of timing, and as it says in the Bible: "There is a time for everything."

Most people are naturally concerned about what will happen and at what time: this year, next year, or ten years from now. Knowledge of timing is of great importance in the strategic planning for life. If people know beforehand what will happen, they are in a strengthened position to take advantage of the upcoming opportunity or to minimize, if not avoid, any upcoming misfortune. Oftentimes, one event—good or bad—in life will have a chain effect on other things. Therefore, it is a blessing to know the timing in which things will happen in life.

To obtain precise information of timing regarding the ups and downs in life, we need to have more detailed tools to get the job done. This is what this chapter is all about.

There are two methods to use: age mapping and season of the year. With age mapping, a specific location on the face relates to a specific age. By analyzing that location, one can foretell a person's fate at that age. With the season of the year method, you can determine what kind of fate you will have in a specific season: spring, summer, autumn, or winter.

Age Mapping

The fathers of Chinese face reading were, amazingly, able to relate these features and locations to specific years in life, making the human face a detailed calendar of fate. For instance, looking at Figure 5.1 on page 39, one can see that the eyebrows correspond with the ages between thirty and thirty-five; the eyes correspond with the ages between thirty-six and forty; the cheekbones tell one's fate around the age of forty-six or forty-seven; while the mouth corresponds with the age of sixty.

Some explanation is in order for using this system of timing. First, the microcosmic structure of the face is symmetrical in that most locations on one side of the face can find their counterparts on the other side, based on an imaginary vertical line dividing the face in two, using the nose as the center.

In Chinese palmistry the left hand is used to foretell a man's fate while the right hand is used for a woman. This divination principle of "male left and female right" is equally applicable in face divination. In all locations and features that are symmetrical with respect to the dividing line, such as the ears, eyes, eyebrows, and cheekbones, the counting of age for a male should begin with the left side of the line, and for a female with the right half. This gives us two different pictures, one for the male (Figure 5.1, page 39) and one for the female (Figure 5.2, page 40).

For instance, the age period between one and seven for a male should start with the left ear, whereas the same age period for a female should start with the right ear. Similarly, the age of thirty falls on the inner corner of the left eyebrow for a male, but on the inner corner of the right eyebrow for a female. It is highly recommended that one commit these two figures to memory if one is serious about becoming a face reader.

Since this micro system of face reading is mainly a time recorder, it does not tell the exact physiognomical meaning of an individual year. To find out what is in store at a specific age, you need to analyze the

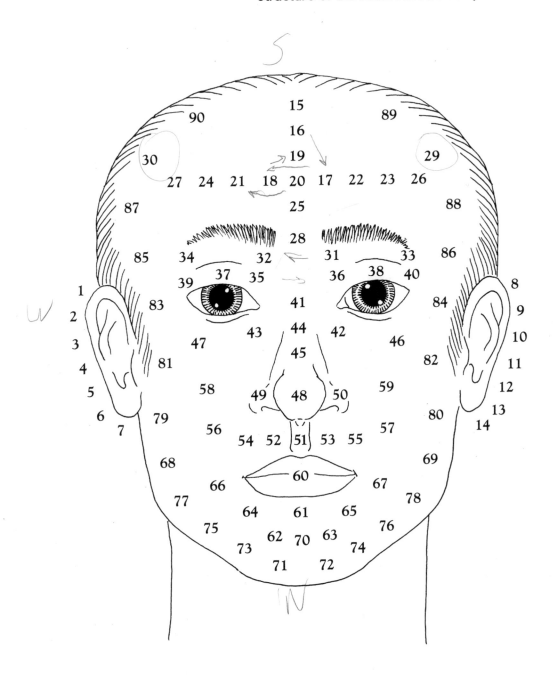

Figure 5.1: Age map for a male

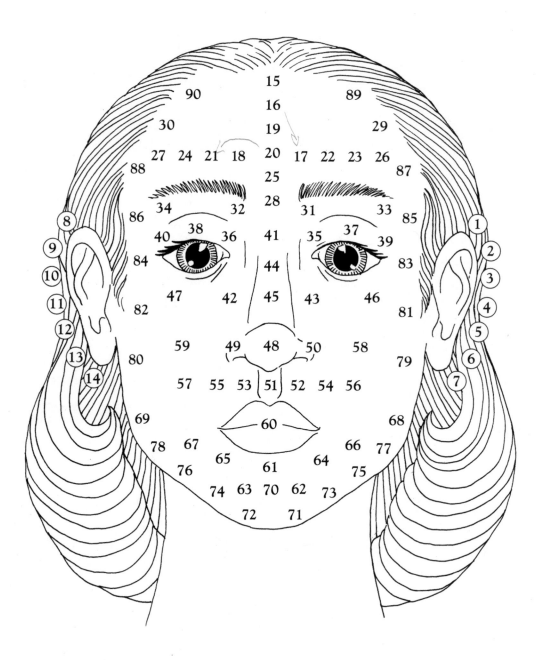

Figure 5.2: Age map for a female

representative facial feature to find out. For instance, the age of thirty-two falls on the inner corner of the left eyebrow. This, in itself, does not tell anything about the fate of the person at that specific age. To find out how the person was, is, or will be faring around that period of time, you will have to master the reading of the eyebrows—what is considered a good, auspicious eyebrow and what is not, etc. (Refer to chapter 10 for more on eyebrows or the specific feature you're interested in.)

Seasons

The micro analysis of the face goes even further. The Chinese have their own way of allocating the four seasons of the year to different facial locations to determine what kind of season one will have in terms of fate. For instance, the center of the forehead stands for summer, while the center of the chin stands for winter, the left cheekbone represents spring, while the right cheekbone represents autumn. This applies to both men and women. (See Figure 5.3, page 42.)

To understand the logic used for allocating the seasons, briefly refresh yourself with the Five Mountains system and the principle of the five elements. For example, looking at the Five Mountains system (see Figure 3.2, page 24), the forehead is likened to Mount Heng in the southern part of the country. Then, looking at the five elements correspondence chart (see Table 2.1, page 13), you see that "south" corresponds to "summer," so therefore, the forehead stands for the summer season.

To determine what kind of season one will have in terms of fate, we need to look at the color and spirit of the related facial feature. This is because as far as one's fate in an individual season is concerned, it is the color and spirit of the facial feature rather than the "land form" of the feature that really matters.

Continuing the example above, the forehead corresponds to the summer season. If the color and spirit surrounding the forehead are very good, then an auspicious summer is projected, even if the forehead itself is not very auspicious. On the other hand, if the color of the forehead appears dark or pale, then summer will be a time of trouble, even if the forehead itself is good.

For more details on color and spirit, you will need to refer to chapter 7. Generally, a bright spirit and a yellow color are considered auspicious because they are based on the norms of the Chinese culture. Adjustments will need to be made for other ethnic groups.

永美命

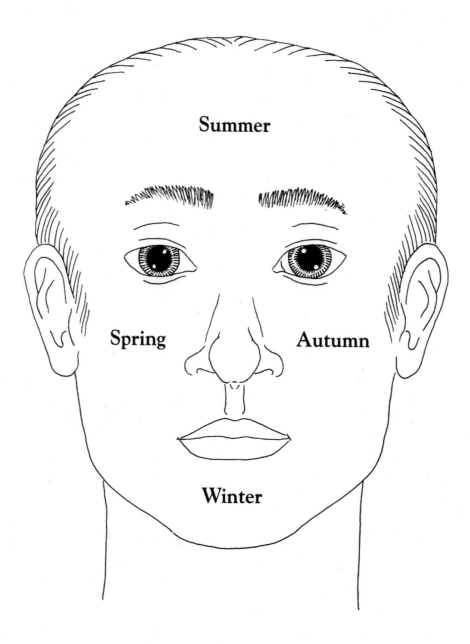

Figure 5.3: Seasons of the face

Chapter 6

Five Basic Face Shapes

Chinese physiognomy classifies the human face into five basic shapes that relate to the five elements: wood, water, metal, fire, and earth. As different as these face shapes are in terms of appearance and personality, they all are auspicious signs of good fortune and happiness. In other words, success is guaranteed for those born with pure basic face shapes, although the timing and areas of success may vary depending on the type.

Unfortunately, not many faces fit exactly into one of these five types. More common are faces that are a combination of two or more basic shapes. While this certainly complicates the task of face reading, there is a way to read them to determine some information about one's fate.

First, let's start with the descriptions for the five basic face shapes.

Wood Face

A wood face projects a general impression of being long and slim. The whole contour of the face is rectangular from forehead to chin. (See Figure 6.1.) Besides being long and rectangular, the face should have a straight nose, long ears, deep lines, and long and slim eyebrows. A wood shape is further confirmed if the person is tall, slim, and straight in stature.

According to the principle of the five elements, wood stands for benevolence and tenacity. So, one born with a wood face is therefore considered to be tenacious, kind, sympathetic, generous with money, and caring about social welfare—the very image of a big tree shielding people from the hot sun or stormy weather.

However, the fate of wood-faced people is not as pleasant as the service they provide to others. Just as a tree, a big tree in particular, has to stand all kinds of extreme weather, a wood-faced person has to work harder than others in order to succeed. Although in the end, their benevolence and tenacity will pay off handsomely. Success is guaranteed for these people, but it comes at a slow pace.

In addition to worldly success, these people will enjoy longevity, for Confucius says:

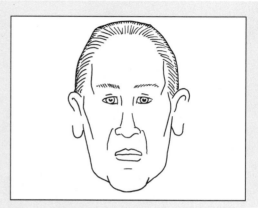

Figure 6.1: Wood face shape

"The kind-hearted people will be compensated with longevity." As another benefit, wood-faced people can be very lucky in terms of money. For instance, many of them do not have to work hard in order to live a materially comfortable life; many are born with silver spoons in their mouths. Others inherit considerable amounts of money from others. Still others may suddenly rise to financial prosperity almost unexpectedly, as in the case of a lottery winner.

Just as trees stretch themselves out in their surroundings, wood-faced people tend to be outgoing and assertive in their efforts and dealings with others. In fact, their inclination towards leadership can be as strong as their desire to help and serve others. These qualities combined can result in a resourcefulness and initiative that would

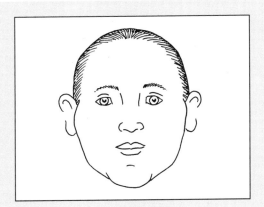

Figure 6.2: Water face shape

water face is quite round and plump, even fat, so much so that one cannot see the bones or depressions in it. (See Figure 6.2.) A genuine water face is further confirmed if the person is short and quite overweight, with a large belly and back.

The very roundness of a water-shaped face is suggestive of a personality as flexible and adaptable as water. Those with water faces are exceptionally skillful in adapting to their circumstances and surviving all kinds of storms in life, professional or financial. In a sense, they are born business people and politicians with excellent survival skills. Not surprisingly, many politicians and businessmen are endowed with such a face. Interestingly, for exactly these same reasons, water-faced people are often accused of being opportunistic and lacking in principles.

Deng Xiaoping, the late leader of China, for instance, possessed a water face. That was one of the reasons why he survived three political purges against him within the Communist Party, in addition to the many risks posed to him by the Nationalist regime, eventually emerging as the supreme leader of modern China. This pragmatic remark of his that has become popular reflects his adaptability: "So long as a cat can catch mice, it is a good cat no matter whether it is white or black."

It is also said that water-faced people are hungry for either power or money. This

benefit many others, especially when a wood-faced person occupies a high social position or is in strong financial shape.

Wood is at its best in the spring season. Therefore, creative ideas and major projects are most likely to be launched in this rejuvenating time of the year. In terms of a career, wood-faced people are best suited for professions closely related to social services, medical services, and scientific research. Indeed, many famous politicians, doctors, and scientists are born with such a face. George Bush, for example, possesses a wood face shape.

Water Face

The outstanding characteristics of this face shape lies in its obvious roundness. The hunger gives them a very strong drive in today's material world, and they often accomplish a great deal in business or politics. Usually, water-faced people are fortunate to taste success early in life. Even early in life, they can achieve a lot and make big names for themselves.

However, masters of face divination warn that if the eyes, ears, or nostrils are not good, their luck will be significantly weakened. This is because the ears, eyes, and nostrils are likened to rivers in face divination, and rivers are where water belongs and gains momentum.

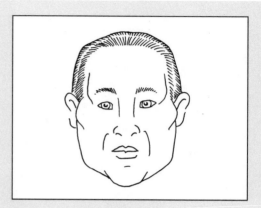

Figure 6.3: Metal face shape

Metal Face

A metal face is one that it is more square than anything else. The bones and flesh are firm and full, the forehead is open and wide, and the mouth and chin are broad and full. (See Figure 6.3.) When compared to a water face, the metal face has more visible bone structure. Since metal corresponds with the color of white, a metal face is further confirmed if it looks white or pale.

The image of metal suggests strength and firmness. These are some of the more outstanding traits in the personality of the metal-faced. Usually, they are upright and outspoken, rarely resorting to flattery and mischief. These qualities help make a metal-faced person a good candidate for a position in the legal/justice field. For the same reason, metal-faced people can easily arouse misunderstanding among colleagues, and unintentionally offend others.

Metal-faced people are entrepreneurial. They are courageous, often short-tempered, but cautious and sometimes calculating. They are inclined to think thrice before they jump. An inborn sense of discretion makes them appear somewhat slow in action and overly cautious at times. You can be sure they are going to read the fine print before signing any document. Their ability to accurately and thoroughly weigh the pros and cons of a situation, together with their foresight, enables them to become firm executors of ideas once they make up their minds.

Despite a sharp temper, a metal-faced person rarely directs his wrath at others in a

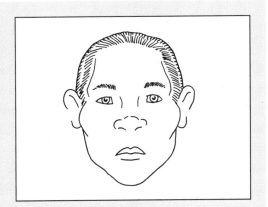

Figure 6.4: Fire face shape

personal way. His anger is more concerned with the issues at hand rather than the people. It is a "clean" sort of anger—without malice or jealousy. Once all the issues have been duly addressed and the necessary measures taken, he or she can then "bury the hatchet" with others, and want to return to the same friendly relationship as before. However, the relationship might have already been damaged. It is, therefore, advisable for metal-faced people to keep in mind the saying that "if toughness is carried too far, it is liable to breakage," and learn to temper their anger with some grace and flexibility.

The metal-faced are born to be leaders, as long as the other features in the face are also good. These people often hold high government or business positions and possess considerable power. It is said that the founding emperors of the Song Dynasty (Zhao Kuanyin) and Yuan Dynasty (Kublai Khan) had metal face shapes.

Fire Face

A fire face features an obviously wider middle portion of the face, with the cheekbones and nose standing out in clear profile—as if commanding respect or fear—and a narrower lower portion of the face, with the jaws and chin receding. (See Figure 6.4.)

Owners of such a face are hardly good-tempered. On the contrary, they are typically hot-headed as the term "fire" indicates. Courageous, ambitious, furious, fierce, and sometimes cruel, fire-shaped people make good soldiers and adventurers. They can become noble and famous during their military careers, especially at a time of war or turmoil. They will fit into any profession that requires extraordinary physical courage, including athletics and boxing.

It is said that the famous scholar and sophisticated face reader, general Zen Guofan, who brutally suppressed the Taiping Rebellion in the mid-nineteenth century, had special favor for the fire-faced in his selection of soldiers and generals. He made it a point in his design of the military echelon—be it a company or a division—that those with fire faces be placed in either the front or the rear of the group, while the other soldiers were placed in the middle. He did this because the front line bears the brunt of the attack from the enemy, and the rear line is most liable to a surprise attack by the enemy. The middle portion of an army is usually the safest place with the least physical risk involved. So those placed in the front and rear of an army needed greater physical courage than those stationed in the middle, so as to handle the greater physical risks with composure and courage—and composure and courage are what finally count in military campaigns. This is especially the case when battles were fought with low-tech weapons like spears and swords. This remains true today in the field of martial arts competition.

According to Chinese philosophy, fire is symbolic of propriety. Therefore, fire-faced people are supposed to be proper in their conduct, and rarely become involved in sexual scandals. Part of the reason is because they are not very knowledgeable about the art of the heart.

Just as fire generates light and warmth, the fire-faced are usually bright and intelligent. They can come up with new, creative ideas easily, but they are not necessarily good ideas. The stumbling blocks of the fire-faced are their ambition and lack of confidence in others. They try to do too many things too quickly, but their lack of confidence in others prevents them from delegating responsibilities. As a consequence, they often overextend themselves. Usually, these people reach the zenith of their career in their middle age, before their energy is spent. For them, old age may be lonely and uncomfortable, either because their spouses or children have died or divorced, or because they have done something they regret.

Earth Face

An earth face strikes others as thick and heavy: a large head, full face, thick eyebrows, fleshy nose and ears, as well as a wide mouth. (See Figure 6.5 on page 49.)

Earth-faced people are more stable in temperament and nature. They move in a steady and stately manner, often appearing quiet, calm, reserved, easy-going, and sometimes even a little slow mentally—but this can be misleading. In reality, they are not as quiet as they may look. They can be tough and demanding, even aggressive and scheming at times. True, they move slowly, but they think things through thoroughly. Oftentimes, a calm, easy-going appearance covers up an unsuitable desire for power and materialistic comforts.

An earth-faced person can be expected to keep a secret. They tend to think twice before opening their mouths, and will try to be as good as their word. In Chinese philosophy, earth is a symbol of trustworthiness.

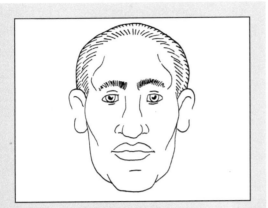

Figure 6.5: Earth face shape

Those born with genuine earth faces are blessed in that money and material comforts come easily to them; they do not have to work hard for these things. They can accumulate a lot of money in their lives. They are usually gifted with a staunch physique and are capable of enjoying good health and longevity—if they know how much is enough in terms of earthly comforts.

When confronted with a face that is a combination of the five basic face shapes, a master of face reading will first try to find out what the dominant face shape is. This means asking whether it is largely a fire, wood, water, metal, or earth shape. Once the dominant shape is determined, a master reader will apply the principle of mutual production and mutual destruction among the five elements to the face being read. For example, if a face is determined to be largely a wood shape, how will the feature from the water-shaped face affect the basic structure? How does that metal feature fit into the broad picture? This process can take a while, but the final conclusion will emerge as a result of a systematic analysis of the face incorporating all the relevant features instead of only one.

For instance, a fundamentally wood-shaped face with a pair of water ears (ears from a water-shaped face) bodes well for the person, even if the face is not a pure wood shape. This is because water can nourish wood in the theory of the five elements. Conclusion: this is a lucky face, and the person will have a fortunate life. On the other hand, if the face is accompanied by a pair of metal ears, the person's good luck will be reduced because metal cuts wood, a destructive relationship in the principle of the five elements. Conclusion: the person will still be lucky due to a close conformity with one of the five basic face shapes, but the good luck will be reduced because of the destructive relationship between metal and wood.

As mentioned earlier, Chinese physiognomy takes into account not only facial features, but non-facial features as well, such as the body structure. This body structure can have an effect on one's fate. The principle of purity in Chinese divination recommends that it is best for a water-shaped face to be situated on a water-shaped body, a wood-shaped face to be found on a wood-shaped body, and so on. If this is the case, the luck of the person will be further enhanced. Otherwise, the luck will be somewhat reduced for the person. The body structures for the basic face shapes are as follows: a water-shaped body is assumed to be round and fat; a fire-shaped body is slim and narrow in the shoulders; a wood-shaped body is tall, slim, and straight; a metal-shaped body looks square and solid, with broad shoulders; and an earth-shaped body is strong and short, with fleshy, muscular legs.

Summary Reading #1: Basic Face Shapes

Test your knowledge on chapter 6. Look at the photo of the popular world figure on the following page and try to read his face, specifically analyzing his face shape. Then see how closely your analysis matches the author's, as well read a full interpretation of this person's fate.

George Bush was the forty-first president of the United States, serving from 1988 to 1992.

George Bush

Face shape:_____

_____

_____

_____

_____

Author's interpretation: Bush has a typical wood face. The dominant feature is its extraordinary length. Indeed, almost every feature in it is long—the long forehead, long nose, long philtrum, and long ears. True to the image of a tree—straightforward, tenacious, and reaching higher and higher—this is a diligent person who is success-oriented and can ascend to the highest position in the country.

Wood-faced people are naturally kind and generous. For all his innate kindness and tolerance, Bush's downward-sloping eyebrows tell me that he can be militant in speech against his political rivals, and resolute in action against the enemies of his country. He has the will and the muscle to remove obstacles standing in his way to success, because success means so much to him.

Bush is a very power-oriented person. In a large sense, he is a born leader. What he likes most is to lead; what he likes least is to be led. This is confirmed by his broad and protruding Career Palace in his forehead, his long and protruding chin, and his impressive character "one" mouth, resembling a straight bar.

It must be said that Bush's strong ambition is well supported by his high intelligence and wisdom as revealed by his auspicious forehead, which is long, deep, and broad. His good luck in politics is indicated by his high and long nose, long and deep philtrum, and his conspicuous Horse Bones, which extend from his cheekbones all the way to his ears. All of these combine in a perfect manner to ensure that he would ascend to the highest government position, leading his country and people to victory and glory.

No doubt, George Bush is lucky. His respectable family background and happy childhood are revealed by his deep, protruding forehead and long, wood ears. This must be a person born with a silver spoon in his mouth. The admirable thing about him is that he was not spoiled by affluence and comfort provided by his family. Instead, he knows how to take advantage of the opportunities provided by his family and mingle them with his own hard work. Moreover, he is determined to elevate his already prominent family background to an even higher level of glory and dignity. This ambitious determination is revealed by the powerful gaze of his eyes. Things have worked out very much the way he had planned.

His political success, though glorious and brilliant, is not the whole story. Equally fortunate is his luck with wealth. While money is not his goal in life, he is born with an above-average, money-making nose and an excellent Property Palace represented by his long, broad, and protruding chin. This reveals that besides the decent salary he earns, he may have inherited some property from his parents. In other words, he must be in possession of some valuable real estate.

While most wood-faced people are able to live a long life, Bush's strong chin ensures that he will not only live a long life, but also enjoy a materially affluent, spiritually fulfilling, and physically healthy old age in a large, warm family. He can live well into his eighties.

Chapter 7

Face Color and Spirit

As intangible and changeable as facial color and spirit are, they are nonetheless important considerations in Chinese face reading. In traditional Chinese medicine, doctors look at the color of a patient's face to help in the diagnosis. They believe that facial color reflects the functions of the internal organs. In divination, color is believed to reflect the fate of a person.

Color and spirit have a higher priority than individual facial features, because they are more instantaneous and changeable. They can change from year to year, season to season, month to month, and even day to day. Since they are so changeable, and also hard to define, the accurate detection of color and spirit surrounding a face becomes one of the most difficult undertakings in face divination. The material in this chapter may be more difficult to learn and apply, so take your time with it. It will be carried over into the other chapters so it is important to learn.

While determining facial color can be fairly explicit, reading one's spirit is much more subtle and intangible. Spirit refers to the entire appearance of a person's face, largely revealed by the eyes and facial color of that person. Just as we say that someone looks in "high spirits," we mean that person seems full of energy, confidence, and enthusiasm. A good spirit is at once a result of strong mental energy as well as the physical qi energy of that person.

Hard to describe, spirit is something that is "felt" more than it is seen, and takes years of experience to read, sometimes only with the help of a "sixth sense." For instance, if a person's eyes look dim (unclear, dark) and drunken, even if the person has not consumed alcohol, an experienced face reader would say that person has a bad, inauspicious spirit. This is because the Chinese fathers hold that a clear spirit is a reflection of a clear mind, which is needed for making sound decisions. Hence, such a spirit is considered an auspicious sign. Therefore, a spirit that looks dull and drunken is considered inauspicious.

Color and spirit have a significant and immediate impact on our luck. Take for example the Spouse Palaces, which are situated at the outer corners of the eyes. If these two small areas look darker than normal, chances are that one of the following things will happen: either the person or his spouse is engaged in an extramarital affair, the relationship between the couple is very strained, or the spouse is seriously ill at this time.

Since color can change quickly and frequently, these troubles are immediate and temporary, usually lasting no more than a week or so, unless the same dark color persists for a long time.

Color and spirit together outweigh the rest of the face. In other words, if the color and spirit are auspicious, one will have good luck for a few days, even if the other facial features are not very auspicious. On the other hand, if the color and spirit are not good, one will have misfortune for several days, even though the rest of the face is auspicious.

An important factor that can affect the changing nature of color and spirit is one's mind—meaning one's thoughts and actions. The traditional Chinese understanding is that the face varies in accordance with one's mind. Good intentions, such as helping others in trouble, especially when the intention and resulting action are kept secret, will bring about favorable changes in one's fortune as reflected in the color and spirit of the face. On the other hand, if one harbors ulterior motives and is intent on hurting others, unfavorable changes in that person's fortune will come about as reflected in their facial color and spirit.

This correlation between intention and fortune has been emphasized and reemphasized by Chinese fathers. It is in line with the theory of reincarnation in which the fate of everybody in the current life is largely determined by his or her own behavior and performance in his or her prior life. As such, the current life is only a link or a continuation in a series of lives, both in the past and in the future. In other words, if we had performed a lot of good deeds in our prior lives, we will be born with very lucky fortunes. On the other hand, if we had committed crimes and misdeeds in our prior lives, we will be punished accordingly in this lifetime by way of bad luck. This is the universal law of nature.

To know what your performance was in your prior life, just look at your fate in the current life. To know what your fate will be in the next lifetime, just summarize your performance (in the moral sense of the word) in your current life. In an absolute sense, we are the masters of our own fate. The power to make our lives happy or miserable ultimately rests on ourselves.

Why is our fate in this lifetime largely, but not completely, determined by our own

behavior in the prior life? To answer this question is to go deep into traditional Chinese philosophy. Chinese ancients believe that while we ourselves are largely responsible for the well-being of our present lives, the behavior of our fathers and grandfathers can also affect our fate. This is the Buddhist teaching of "reward or punishment through generations," which the Chinese take seriously. This means that in whatever we do, we should think in terms of reward and punishment not only for ourselves, but also for our family members and offspring. If one does not have a spouse or children, this situation itself is considered a punishment, and a serious one at that, since the Chinese are a very family-oriented people and care a lot about the continuation of the family tree and the well-being of their children.

An example of "reward or punishment through generations" is illustrated in a story of Chinese folklore, a story scary enough to send a chill down the nerves of most Chinese people. Bai Qi was a top general for the Beginning Emperor of Qin Dynasty (265–420 B.C.). He secretly buried alive 400,000 enemy troops who surrendered to him, presumably at the order of the emperor. To punish Bai Qi for his treacherous act and utter cruelty, God reincarnated all of his offspring into a family of ants.

When preparing to read a person's facial color and spirit, there are several tips to keep in mind. First, do not stand too close to the person; keep a distance so as to be more objective. A good distance is about two feet, but usually no more than three feet. If you are too close to the person being read, the person may feel nervous and strained, and their facial color and spirit may change as a result. This cannot but affect the accuracy of your reading, which you want to avoid.

Other tips include not letting sunlight directly shine on the face; keep the person calm and relaxed; and don't read anyone who is under the influence of alcohol or overly sleepy. It is fairly common knowledge that facial complexion can be seriously affected by a dramatic change in mood or emotion, as well as when under the influence of alcohol. Alcohol can cause the face to redden quickly—the same way it does when one becomes angry or upset. This is not the genuine color of the face, but the result of temporary, unnatural influences.

The best time for someone to have a color reading is immediately after getting up in the morning. It is believed that this is the time of the day when one's facial color is at its truest, when they are the least affected by external factors and internal emotions.

If the person's current facial color is a result of artificial means such as tanning, then no reading can be made based on color. If the person wants, ask him or her to come back after their natural skin color has returned. Chinese face reading should be conducted under the most natural circumstances possible if a high degree of accuracy is desired.

Spirit

As mentioned before, to read a person's spirit, one needs a lot of experience. This is similar to that of a doctor diagnosing a patient, especially a Chinese doctor. By looking at a patient's face, i.e. his spirit, an experienced, seasoned Chinese doctor can tell many things: whether the patient is suffering from a recently contracted disease or has had it for a long time; whether the patient is better or worse than the last doctor visit; or whether the case is life-threatening or not.

The same logic applies to a face reader. My advice is to look at both the facial color and the eyes, because these are the two places where one's spirit is most revealed.

Spirit is considered the most important aspect of a face because it affects our fate most directly and immediately. It is a priority in face reading and should be one of the first things to look at, giving us a quick forecast of our immediate fate. It should then be combined with the reading of the facial color. When combining, more weight is given to the spirit reading (60 percent) than to the facial color (40 percent).

For example, favorable spirit in a face appears clear, bright, strong, profound, or steady. If a person appears clear minded, in high spirits, and in a stable mood, it indicates a favorable spirit. Nothing bad or disastrous will come to the person in the next ten days or so. If the facial color is then determined to be unfavorable, the person will still not encounter anything bad or unlucky. Therefore, the favorable spirit outweighed the unfavorable facial color.

An unfavorable spirit is considered dark, dull, superficial, or shaky. For instance, if a person appears sleepy, drunken, out of sorts, or simply very tired or depressed, you can tell that the person does not have an auspicious spirit. A person low in spirit is often found sick and in trouble. Sickness itself is a form of ill luck, if you agree with Emerson that health is the greatest wealth and happiness. In such a case, no favorable color can last long when spirit is unfavorable.

In addition, spirit is reflected in the manner in which one carries oneself—the way in which one speaks and laughs, sits and walks, eats and drinks. For instance, a person full of spirit will most likely be optimistic in attitude, sonorous in voice (as if the voice comes directly out of the lower abdomen), sitting straight, or walking in big, steady strides. If one is low in spirit, one will be pessimistic, talk in a weak voice, be short of breath, leaning on chair or sofa, or less steady in walking.

Color

While there are standard facial colors identified as auspicious or inauspicious, they are simplified generalizations. For instance, violet, yellow, and sanguine are typically good colors while dark and green are typically unlucky colors. The final conclusion as to the normal or auspicious color will have to be determined by analyzing several other factors.

These factors include the correspondence to the five elements, including face shape, geographic location, and ethnic background (skin color), the age of the person, and the season of the year when the reading is done. Once those are looked at, you can then determine the length of the good or bad luck seen in the color or spirit.

Remember: As with all the other areas of face reading, while there is somewhat of an order or process, it is not a clear step-by-step approach. Instead, it is necessary to look at all the factors involved and then combine them to make a final analysis.

The facial colors described here, such as violet, yellow, or green, are literal colors, where you actually *see* that color, tone, or shade in the complexion of the person. The color will not always be obvious or explicit, which again points to the difficulty of reading facial color and how experience makes a difference. Also, when referring to the color black, it means "dark," where the skin is darker than what is normal, not literally black. It does not refer to any ethnic group.

It is also important to note that "normal" or "auspicious" colors given throughout this chapter—and this book—are based on the norms of the Asian ethnic group. For instance, yellow is considered one of the normal colors partly because the Chinese refer to themselves as the "yellow race." Adjustments will need to be made based on your own ethnic background and its norms or standards.

To begin reading facial color, analyze the various factors listed to determine what the normal color is for that person. Then we can correctly interpret their fate.

Five elements: The principle of the five elements, its correspondences to face shape and geographic location, and the theory of mutual production and destruction are all important determinants of color. (Refer to chapter 2 to refresh your memory on these terms.)

First, look at the *face shape*. For example, referring to the table of correspondences on page 13, the corresponding color for a water-shaped face is black (dark). Therefore, such a person should have a slightly darker complexion. Similarly, if a person has a wood-shaped face, green is considered the natural color of wood, so the person should possess a greener complexion than others.

Continuing to look at the table of correspondences, find the *geographic location* for that person. For example, people from the north are supposed to have darker complexions than others, since north corresponds with the element of water, which has a normal color of black (dark). People from the south are supposed to have a brighter color, since south corresponds with the element of fire, which has red as its normal color.

Now you need to combine these two factors. For example, what would happen to a person with a fire-shaped face (corresponding color of red), who has a dark complexion? Obviously, this is not an auspicious sign, for the dark complexion corresponds with water, which is the conqueror of fire, based on the theory of mutual destruction. You can then expect misfortune falling on the person around the time the reading is conducted. (Remember: color is of a temporary nature and usually indicates things happening within a week or so.)

However, if this person is also from the south, then the combined fire element (fire-shaped face corresponds with the southern location) outweighs the water element (dark complexion). The result: just some frustration instead of misfortune.

The same logic of mutual destruction applies to a water-shaped face with a yellow complexion (earth stops water), a metal-shaped face with a red complexion (fire melts metal), or a wood-shaped face with a white complexion (metal cuts wood).

If the relationship is mutual production rather than mutual destruction, the result is more positive. A wood-shaped face (normal color of green) with a dark complexion is divined to be a favorable sign of luck because water (corresponds with dark complexion) nourishes wood. Similarly, it is good for a fire-shaped face to have a green complexion (wood feeds fire), a water-shaped face to have a white complexion (metal generates water), an earth-shaped face to have a red complexion (fire begets earth), and a metal-shaped face to have a yellow complexion (earth produces metal).

If a face does not fit completely into one of the five basic face shapes, we cannot stretch the rules to fit. Simply ignore this factor of the five elements and use the other principles and rules.

If a face does have a dominant but not very pure face shape, that dominant shape should be the basis of your analysis. For example, a largely metal-shaped face may have a red facial color. Since red represents fire, which destroys metal (mutual destruction), we can determine that the person has wealth and social position thanks to the auspicious metal face shape, but the person's wealth will not be very big, nor will the social position be very high, simply because the red facial color, representing the

destructive fire element, spoils or reduces the otherwise good luck of the face shape.

In an example of mutual production, if a person's face shape is dominantly wood, but the person possesses a thick, fleshy chin—the image of water—then we can say that his or her luck will only be further enhanced, because water nourishes wood.

We also need to take into account the *ethnic background* of the person. The correspondence chart and its "normal" colors are all based on Chinese standards. When applying these factors to other ethnic groups, the "normal" colors will need to be adjusted based on your ethnic group's standards. For example, for Caucasians or fair-skinned people, white can take the place of yellow as the normal, auspicious color. For black-skinned people, black would then become the normal, and therefore, auspicious color, while white and yellow would be considered inauspicious for them. Similarly, for brown-skinned people, brown would be the normal and auspicious color, with black and white being inauspicious colors for them.

Age: The next factor to look at to determine a person's normal color is the age of the person. As one advances in age, one's facial color and spirit also change. Fathers of face divination have determined the normal, auspicious facial colors for specific age groups: light (clear) for a child, bright (illuminating) for a young adult, rosy for the middle-aged, and plain (not illuminating) for the elderly.

Now let's continue to combine this with the factors of the five elements. For example, if a middle-aged person (rosy) has a wood-shaped face (green) but their complexion is white (metal), it tells us that the person does not have an auspicious facial color. This is because white is the color of metal, the element that cuts into wood (mutual destruction). The person will still be lucky, but not as lucky as if the color was green or red (the corresponding normal colors), in the sense that either the person will not climb very high up the career ladder, or their prominent career will be cut short before they reach retirement age. The person will also very likely have some health problems, specifically with the liver, since wood, which corresponds with the liver organ, is "damaged" by metal (from the white complexion).

The auspicious facial color for this person should either be green or rosy because green is the basic color, since the person has a wood-shaped face. Since the relationship between the elements wood and fire is one of mutual production, rosy or red (representing fire) would also be an auspicious color for the person. If this were the case, the fate of that person would be much more positive: lucky, healthy, and wealthy.

Season: Face divination has also determined that facial color varies with the seasons. Whatever the season is when the face reading is done, that is the normal color to look for. For example, spring corresponds with the element of wood, which corresponds with the color green, so people are supposed to possess more or less of a green complexion in the springtime. Continuing on with the other seasons: summer correlates with fire, so we are supposed to have more or less of a red color (ruddy) in summer; autumn corresponds with metal, so we are supposed to look lighter or paler in autumn than other seasons; and winter corresponds with water, so it is perfectly normal that our complexion looks darker in the winter than in other times of the year. This set of rules is independent of what shape of face you have.

Continuing our previous example: if the middle-aged person (rosy) has a wood-shaped face (green) with a white complexion, and the reading is done in the wintertime, this scenario reveals that, at least for the time being, there will not be major trouble for the person. This determination is made because that while white is a bad color for the wood-shaped face, the damage represented by the white color will be significantly reduced in the winter, since metal (white) can be melted into water (winter), which in turn nourishes the wood.

Here we see a roundabout beneficial relationship instead of a direct one.

After taking into account all the factors of face shape, geographic location, ethnicity, and season, the determined normal color for this person is rosy or green.

Length of Luck

Now that we know the person's spirit and normal color, let's find out the length of the good or back luck revealed by these two dimensions.

There are three aspects to look at: clear versus dim, implicit versus explicit, and old versus young.

If the color is clear-cut rather than vague, it is a sign that something—good or bad—is currently happening or ongoing. For instance, if white is an inauspicious color for a person, and such a color appears clearly on that person's face, it is an indication that misfortune is befalling on the person. However, if the color is dim or faint, it means that some related thing is already over. To continue the example, if the white color shows dimly or vaguely on the person's face, the bad luck for that person may well be over, leaving only a mark on the face.

An implicit color is simply a color that is not very clear. While it appears in the face in the same way as an explicit color, the differences lies in the clarity of the color itself.

When a color is implicit, it is a sign that the good or bad things are not over yet. For instance, if the ears appear faintly dark, one must be suffering from kidney disease. However, if the color is explicit, it shows that the good or bad things are almost over.

An old color means a color that is deep and profound, while a young color means one that is only superficial. A color is superficial when beneath it you can detect another color, for instance, a white/pale color beneath a red color. An old color means the luck, good or bad, will last a long time, while a young color indicates the luck will last only a short time.

For example, if a color is favorable and old, such as a deep red color on a fire-shaped person, the person will have very lucky things happen, which will last a long time. If, however, the color is favorable but young, such as a faint red color beneath a white complexion, the person will have only slightly lucky things happen, which will not last very long.

The same principle applies to unfavorable colors. Thus, if one's facial color is unfavorable and old, the person will have a persistently unlucky fate for quite a long time. If the unfavorable color is young, the setbacks will be temporary and losses relatively small.

Applying Color

Once a person's normal color is determined, it can then be applied to individual facial features.

For example, three facial locations are of great significance in terms of color. One is the space between the eyebrows known as the Life Palace, second is the nose tip representing the Wealth Palace, and third are the temples known as the Travel Palaces.

The reason these three locations are considered important is suggested by the name of these palaces. Ask yourself these questions: Is life important to you? If yes, the Life Palace matters a lot as a logical consequence. Is money important to you? If yes, then the Wealth Palace counts a lot. This palace affects your business deals and money prospects. As for the Travel Palaces, they have great impact on our fortune as they can tell if we should travel or not. Many Asians see a face reader simply because they want to know whether or not they should travel for the time being.

If these three locations are bright, yellow, rosy, or your determined normal color, good luck will come in the near future. However, if these three locations are dark, gray, or your inauspicious color, misfortune is going to appear in a short time. To minimize the misfortune, you should stay at home, praying or meditating.

In general, bad facial color can temporarily decrease the luck of a person, turning an otherwise good fortune into a misfortune for a short time, while good facial color can temporarily enhance a person's luck, bringing at least some glory and fortune.

This effect exerted by different colors over one's fate is most obvious in the eyes and the nose. If the eyes are perceived to be dark and dim, it is a sure sign of ill health and ill luck, often turning out to be life-threatening. If the same colors appear in the nose, the bad effect is doubled and the coming of the misfortune is hastened. If the upper portion of the nose bridge suddenly turns white, it is a signal of money losses. If it turns white in the middle portion of the nose, legal trouble is in sight, which often ends in a prison term. If the white color suddenly appears in the nose tip, it indicates fights with others. These could be in the form of lawsuits, financial problems, traffic accidents, or health crises.

Good facial color can enhance the luck of a person, bringing the person at least temporary glory and fortune. For example, since the nose is the Wealth Palace, wealthy people usually have a big, round, fleshy nose. However, some people who make a lot of money do not have such a nose. This is because the color of their noses must be very good during the period in which they are making money. The pity is that such good fortune usually does not last long; indeed, it can be as fluctuating as the color.

Reading Color and Spirit

1. **Determine spirit**
   - Favorable spirit: clear, bright, profound, or steady
   - Unfavorable spirit: dark, dull, superficial, or shaky.
2. **Determine normal color**
   - Face shape
   - Geographic location
   - Ethnicity
   - Age
   - Season
3. **Combine** spirit reading with determined normal color
4. **Determine length of luck** revealed by the combination of color and spirit
   - Clear vs. dim
   - Implicit vs. explicit
   - Old vs. young
5. **Apply determined normal color** to individual features to reveal more information about one's fate

Chapter 8

福 **Ears**

This is the logical starting point for a discussion of the face because according to Chinese physiognomy, the counting of human life begins with the ears. The ears account for the first fourteen years of life.

A fascinating story documented in a Chinese history book describes Liu Bei, the emperor of Shu Kingdom (A.D. 160–223), as having ears that were so long that they "touched his shoulders." Fathers of face divination took this as confirmation of his "Mandate of Heaven," the God-given authority to rule a nation.

With little exception, the facial characteristics of an emperor—particularly that of a founding emperor—are always considered auspicious and have been used as yardsticks for Chinese face reading. Thus, long, thick, and large ears are signs of good fortune. As you enter a Buddhist temple, you will immediately notice that all Buddhas have exceptionally long ears with thick and heavy earlobes. Since Buddhas are the givers of good luck, people resembling Buddha in appearance are considered lucky and prosperous.

Along with good ears being large, thick, and long with fleshy earlobes, there are several other criteria in the evaluation of the ears: location, position, ear door size, and color.

Location: Where the ears are located in relation to the eyebrows is important. Chinese face reading observes that ears extending above the eyebrow level are a very auspicious sign, indicating that the person is highly intelligent and ambitious, had a fortunate childhood, and will have a high social position in life. Typically, people with such ears will start their brilliant career early in life and have huge success. A good example is found in Lin Biao (1906-1971), the youngest and arguably ablest of the ten marshals in Communist China. Lin had many extraordinary facial features. Among other things, Lin (the "devil of war" according to Chiang Kai-shek) had long, flat ears that towered well above his extremely bushy eyebrows. Chiang Kai-shek, Lin's teacher

and political enemy, also possessed such a pair of ears.

Position: Another dimension of the quality of the ear lies in whether it is flat against the head or protruding forward. If both ears lie flat against the head, it is an auspicious sign, indicating that one will win respect from others, that one's orders will be followed, and that one does not have to work hard in order to earn a living. However, if both ears lean forward (push outward) at the top, one will have to work hard to gain respect from others; even one's subordinates will dare to openly argue with him or disregard his orders. The person's life will also be more turbulent, unstable, and full of ups and downs.

Ear door size: The ear door is the opening in the lower corner of the ear's inner circle. (See Figure 8.8 on page 73.) A wide ear door, capable of holding a finger, is considered by Chinese face readers to be preferable, because it indicates an open mind, wide knowledge, spiritual and material generosity, as well as a long life. Such people love to learn and experience different cultures and even different religions. They are more willing to offer financial help, being less concerned about their own pocket than their counterparts with narrow ear doors. Such a personality may account for their potential to live longer than those with narrow ear doors, because they take a longer view of life, have wider interests, and less worries, spiritually and financially.

A narrow ear door, one that you cannot put a finger in, indicates a narrow mind that is prejudicial, vengeful, and stingy. The person oftentimes harbors a strong desire for revenge, remembering even the slightest offenses done to them by others. This cannot but consume a lot of one's life energy, for no good purpose.

Color: The color of the ears also carries heavy significance. White and red are the best colors for ears. Two men as youths had face readers tell them that they would be known throughout the world by virtue of their literary talents. This was because both possessed ears that were whiter than their faces. One of them, Li Bai, later became one of the greatest Chinese poets, and the other, Ou Yangxiu, one of the greatest literary men in China.

Since white and red are typically good colors for ears, black or dark are considered a bad colors. Dark ears usually symbolize illiteracy, poor health, and an unhappy childhood, as well as low intelligence. If the ears suddenly become much darker than the face, it is a warning of an upcoming serious medical condition or legal problem.

Remember: As a general rule, good ears are thick, long, flat, and rise above the eyebrows, with wide doors and fleshy earlobes. If deficiencies exists such as a depression in the ear, or a lack of a clear inner circle, these are sure signs that the person has had or will have serious health problems before the age of five.

Different shapes of ears have different meanings. They provide reliable clues to the personality of people and their fortune early in life, during the ages of one to fourteen.

On the following pages are various types of ears and their interpretations.

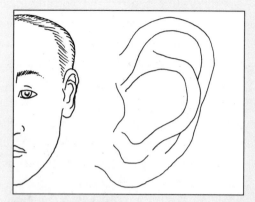

Figure 8.1: Metal ears

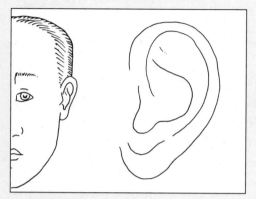

Figure 8.2: Wood ears

Metal Ears

Metal ears are thick, white, close against the head, and stand higher than eyebrow level, with distinct contours of the inner and outer circles. (See Figure 8.1.) Such ears indicate great intelligence, national fame, and a high social position, in addition to a happy childhood resulting from a good family background. Those with metal ears are bound to cut a conspicuous figure in their chosen field or profession, be it art, literature, politics, or business. Their success comes at an early age, usually before thirty, especially when such ears are set on a metal- or water-shaped face.

Wood Ears

Wood ears are protruding, obviously wider at the upper part, with a more prominent outer circle than inner circle. (See Figure 8.2.) Wood ears signify wealth, intelligence, and longevity. Usually, people with wood ears are born into well-to-do families, and possess strong artistic and aesthetic tastes. These people do not need to worry about their livelihood, as their basic material needs will be well taken care of. If they decide to pursue a career in art or science, the chances are great that they will meet with rewarding success. Such ears are best set on a wood- or water-shaped face to be the most auspicious. If found on an earth-shaped face, the luck and fortune of the owner will be reduced.

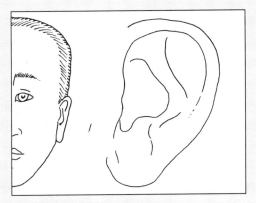

Figure 8.3: Water ears

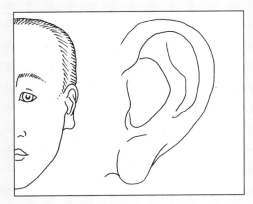

Figure 8.4: Earth ears

Water Ears

Water ears are thick, long, and flat, with big, fleshy earlobes that extend lower than the nose tip (See Figure 8.3.) Water ears indicate power, authority, wealth, honor, and extraordinary fame. Owners of water ears, if their face is of a water- or metal-shape, can often climb to the top in a military or political career. This often comes late in life, typically after the age of fifty.

Earth Ears

Earth ears are long and thick, with big earlobes that lean forward toward the mouth, as if guarding the face. (See Figure 8.4.) Such ears signify wealth, fame, a good career, and longevity. Owners of earth ears can hold high government positions if their eyes and noses are also good. They are great lovers of both food and women. They are born to be lucky in that they will always have plenty to eat wherever they go and find it easy to attract members of the opposite sex.

Fire Ears

Fire ears are the opposite of water ears. While water ears are typically wider on the top, fire ears are wider at the bottom with more pointed ear tops. (See Figure 8.5, page 72.) Fire ears indicate intelligence, wealth, propriety, obedience to the law, and great success in the later stages of life. Typically, owners of fire ears have a devoted wife, a

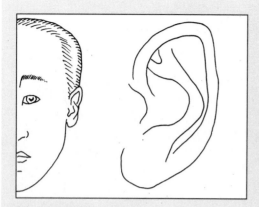

Figure 8.5: Fire ears

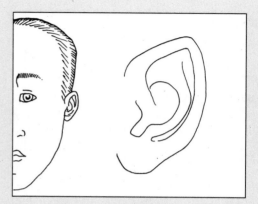

Figure 8.6: Mouse ears

harmonious family, and a happy old age. On the negative side, they tend to be overcautious, sensitive, and sometimes suspicious of others. Therefore, they may have many enemies and will be seen as picky bosses.

Mouse Ears

Mouse ears are small and somewhat protruding and pointed at the top. (See Figure 8.6.) Such ears tell an experienced face reader that their owner had a hard childhood, either because of family troubles or health problems. They are frugal, sometimes to the point of stinginess, as well as opportunistic and calculating. Fathers of face reading tell us that those with mouse ears will have to work harder than others in order to succeed and enjoy good health.

They may, if not careful, suffer from a violent death during middle age unless their nose and the lower portion of the face are auspicious; then they can avoid such misfortune and live to a comfortable old age.

Pig Ears

Pig ears are large but thin and soft, with the whole ear protruding forward and lacking distinctive inner circles. (See Figure 8.7, page 73.) Pig ears are inauspicious in that they signify a life with a lot of hard work but not much profit, frequent travel (not a good thing in traditional Chinese society, which values a stable family life), loss of money or bankruptcy, lack of authority and respect from others, and an eventful life, full of ups and downs in fortune. They seem

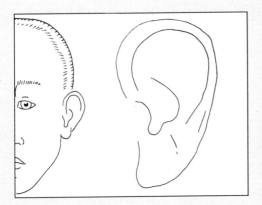

Figure 8.7: Pig ears

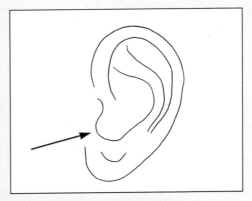

Figure 8.8: Ears with wide doors

to be running all the time, with little rest or leisure time; to get the same result requires double the effort of those more fortunate.

Ears with Wide Doors

If an ear door can hold one finger or more, it is considered a wide door. (See Figure 8.8.) Such ears indicate intelligence, longevity, generosity, and open-mindedness. These people are less tight with their money when helping others. They are quick to learn, more open to new ideas and thinking, make friends easily, and will assume a democratic management style if they happen to be leaders. They also tend to be very energetic and live long lives, especially if hair grows in the ears.

Ears with Narrow Doors

If an ear door cannot hold a finger, it is considered a narrow door. (See Figure 8.9, page 74.) Such ears suggest that their owners are more narrow-minded, conservative, stingy, and secretive. Their lives tend not to be very long either. Many rich business people are born with such ears. They generally follow the motto: If you take care of the penny, dollars will take care of themselves. Fortunately, if the eyes are good and large, and the eyebrows set wide apart, owners of ears with narrow doors are still capable of generosity in terms of thinking and money.

Ears with Big Earlobes

These ears have fleshy, long earlobes that hang on the ears. (See Figure 8.10, page

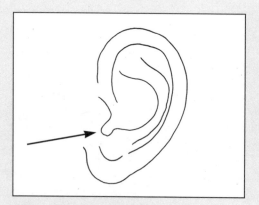

Figure 8.9: Ears with narrow doors

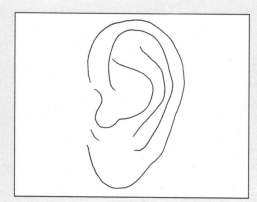

Figure 8.10: Ears with big earlobes

74.) They signify good luck in materialistic and sexual comforts. In a word, big earlobes are an indication of happiness. Owners of such ears are either very lucky in family life with satisfactory spouses, or have many sexual encounters throughout their lives. They are almost bound to marry, perhaps more than once, but they possibly have extramarital affairs. They do not have to work very hard in order to secure their basic needs and their relationship with their parents is generally very good.

Ears with Small Earlobes

If the earlobes are thin and short, they are considered small earlobes. (See Figure 8.11, page 75.) Ears with small lobes signify mis-

fortune in relationships and sexual life. Owners of such ears have a distant relationship with their parents. They usually have a strained relationship, if only for a certain period of life, with their spouse or sex partner. Also, they have to work harder in order to achieve the same amount of career success as those with big earlobes.

Rectangular Ears

These ears look similar to the shape of a rectangle, with distinct corners at the top and bottom. (See Figure 8.12, page 75.) Rectangular ears signify intelligence, wealth, power, high social position, and a big family. They also indicate strong leadership skills.

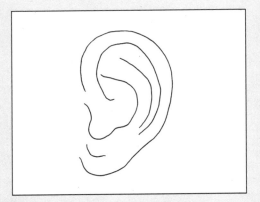

Figure 8.11: Ears with small earlobes

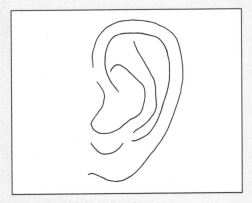

Figure 8.12: Rectangular ears

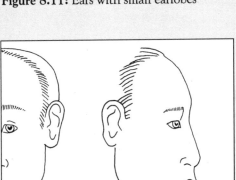

Figure 8.13: High-set ears

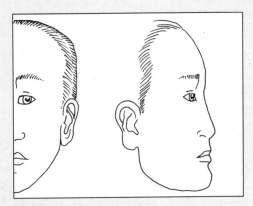

Figure 8.14: Low-set ears

High-set Ears

The tops of these ears rise above the level of the eyebrows. (See Figure 8.13.) This is a clear indication of high intelligence, longevity, an early rise to political power before the age of thirty, and a guarantee against poverty throughout life.

Low-set Ears

Low-set ears extend below the level of the nose. (See Figure 8.14.) They indicate strong determination, perseverance, and longevity. People with these ears will have strong good luck late in life—usually after the age of sixty. However, they often have

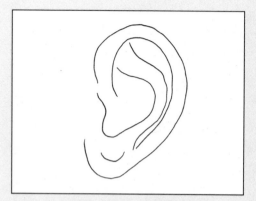

Figure 8.15: Ears with prominent circles

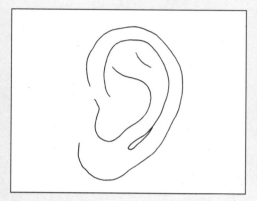

Figure 8.16: Ears with prominent outer circles

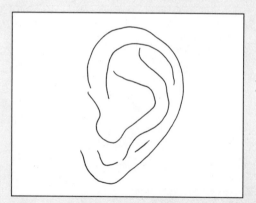

Figure 8.17: Ears with prominent inner circles

Ears with Prominent Circles

There are two circles to each ear: an inner circle and an outer circle. In face reading, the inner circle stands for drive and ambition (political and commercial ambition, in particular), while the outer circle stands for intelligence and health.

Preferably, both circles should be prominent and outstanding. (See Figure 8.15.) Such a person will be highly ambitious and intelligent, full of drive, energy, and confidence.

Ears with Prominent Outer Circles

If the outer circle is more prominent than the inner one (see Figure 8.16), the person is more talented than ambitious. Those with such ears are very likely to excel in art and science.

to marry twice. If the chin is also good, their good luck will be further enhanced in the later part of their life. In Chinese parlance, they will have a brilliant sunset in life, which will handsomely compensate them for their hard work and misfortune in their earlier days.

	Location	Position	Door	Color
Auspicious	above the eyebrow level	flat	wide	white, red
Inauspicious	—	leaning forward	narrow	black, dark

Table 8.1: Summary of criteria for ears

Ears with Prominent Inner Circles

If the inner circle is more outstanding than the outer one (see Figure 8.17, page 76), the person is more ambitious and aggressive than intelligent and healthy. Typically, such a person is inclined to get involved in politics and business, and would pursue success in these fields to the neglect of many other valuable things in life, such as friendship and peace of mind.

Chapter 9

Forehead

A lot of information and life secrets are hidden in the part of the face referred to as the upper portion, or "heaven": childhood happiness, intelligence, mental ability (including memory, logical reasoning, imagination, and intuition), and social position.

The happiness of one's childhood depends largely on family background, and the forehead reveals a lot about this, typically the career, wealth, and social position of the parents as well as the relationship between the parents—whether or not they have a good marriage. One can be born into a rich family, but the relationship between the parents may still be sour and unhappy.

A good forehead informs us that the person comes from a good family background where at least one of the parents makes good money, has a good career, or has inherited a considerable amount of wealth, most likely from the grandparents. This makes a happy childhood possible, which is also free of financial worries. If the ears are also good, then in addition to a good family background, the person is also endowed with a strong physique.

High intelligence is also symbolized in a good forehead. People with good foreheads are gifted with learning ability, strong memory, communication skills, and imaginative power. In fact, many prodigies are found to possess excellent foreheads.

Unfortunately, not all who are born with good foreheads are able or willing to explore their genetic advantage to the fullest. An easy childhood and material comforts may lead some of them astray. Some may just scatter away their energies and waste their talents in mischievous ways. This is why Chinese sages warn that early and easy success in life is a great misfortune in disguise.

What, then, determines a good forehead? Here, we go back to the principle of yin and yang where the criteria differ for males and females. It has nothing to do with equal opportunity between the two genders, but everything to do with fate.

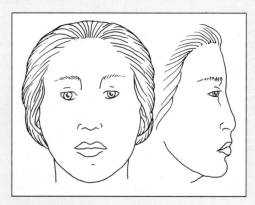

Figure 9.1: Female forehead

Female Forehead

A good forehead is one that is smooth and sanguine, slightly rounded but not protruding, not too high or shallow, and not too broad or narrow. (See Figure 9.1.) It should also not occupy more than one third of the entire face, and no bones should be visible. A female with such a forehead is lucky in that she most likely has been born into a good family and enjoyed her early years. She is intelligent and gentle in temper, loved by all in the family, and appreciated by teachers and classmates in school during her childhood years.

A forehead that is too broad or high is considered an auspicious sign for a man, but it is not recommended for a woman, traditionally. While a sure sign of excellent

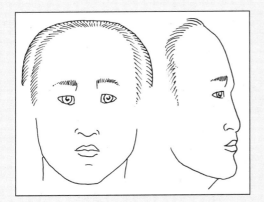

Figure 9.2: Male forehead

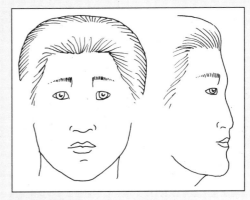

Figure 9.3: Inauspicious forehead

intelligence and good family background for both sexes, in the past such a forehead set on a female face was interpreted by traditional Chinese physiognomy as an indication of marital misfortune. She will marry at least twice if she chooses to marry, and there is a great chance that her husbands will die early in life, not long after they marry. In other words, such a woman is traditionally viewed as bringing bad luck to her husband. Today, a high, broad forehead in a woman is a sign of intelligence, broadmindedness, and the ability to speak her own mind.

Male Forehead

The best forehead for a man is one that is very broad and deep, high and protruding, with visible bones, and that occupies more than one-third of the face. (See Figure 9.2.) A man with such a forehead is very bright, intelligent, ambitious, goal-oriented, and has a good family who he benefits from a lot. Typically, a man with protruding bones in his forehead is also destined to enjoy a high social position. He will have a successful career early in life, typically starting in his early twenties, usually making his living by the use of his mind instead of his hands. This is especially true when the forehead is longer than the chin, the lower portion of the face. As Confucius says: "Those who use their mental power for living rule others, while those who use their physical strength for living are ruled by others." No wonder most leaders in almost all areas of human endeavor are born with such a fore-

	Female	Male
Auspicious	smooth rounded balanced sanguine	high (more than 1/3 of face) broad protruding visible bones
Inauspicious	visible bones too broad or narrow too high or low bumps, moles or lines	low (less than 1/3 of face) narrow or shallow pointed bumps, moles or lines

Table 9.1: Summary of criteria for foreheads

head. Examples include former Chinese leaders Chiang Kai-shek, Mao Tse-tung, and Deng Xiaoping, former U. S. President George Bush, French President Jacques Chirac, and Pope John II.

Inauspicious Forehead

If the forehead is narrow, pointed, or shallow, dotted with bumps or indentations, wrinkles (lines), or moles, not only is mental ability seriously limited, the owner of such a forehead is destined to have a hard and even miserable childhood. (See Figure 9.3, page 81.) Typically, such a person comes from a poor family with a childhood haunted by financial strains and relational crises. There is a great chance that the parents are divorced or separated, leaving them in a broken family. The person may also encounter a physical threat early in childhood, due either to disease or an accident.

Summary Reading #2: Ears and Forehead

Test your knowledge on chapters 8 and 9. Look at the photo of the popular world figure on the following page and try to read his face, specifically analyzing his ears and forehead. Then see how closely your analysis matches the author's interpretation.

Prince Charles is the twenty-first Prince of Wales, the eldest son of Queen Elizabeth II, and heir to the British throne.

Prince Charles of Wales

Ears: _____

_____

_____

_____

_____

Forehead: _____

_____

_____

_____

Author's interpretation: Looking at the forehead and ears, these are two locations that hold most of the secrets about one's family background and early fate.

What marks Charles' forehead are the three horizontal, continuous lines parallel to each other. Fathers of Chinese physiognomy tell us that these lines are indicative of great power, honor, and nobility. This conforms well with the birthrights of His Royal Highness: he is the heir to one of the loftiest positions in the world determined by heredity, and successor to one of the world's greatest private fortunes. To be sure, the odds of being born into his fate are very, very meager. In addition to the title of Prince of Wales for which he is largely known, Charles Philip Arthur George is also the called the Earl of Chester, the Earl of Carrick, the Duke of Cornwall, the Duke of Rothesay, Lord of the Isles, Prince and Great Steward of Scotland, and is the president or a significant patron of hundreds of charitable clubs, committees, and organizations.

However, we cannot say that Charles has a perfect forehead. For a family background as noble as his, one should expect a broader, higher forehead than his. His narrow forehead indicates a lonely personality and emotional trouble. He seems to have few true friends, and has spent most of his life in the company of people outside of his peer group. This cannot but negatively affect his emotional, social, and marital lives. For one thing, he remained a bachelor living with his parents until the age of thirty-three. For another, his marriage to Diana Spencer seemed to run into trouble almost right after the wedding ceremony and long before his formal divorce with Diana.

Indeed, few outsiders can learn to feel at home with the palace lifestyle Charles is accustomed to. While superbly comfortable in a materialistic sense, living the life of a royal can be a life of social and personal imprisonment. Princess Diana's life seemed to be proof of this. Considering that marriage can constitute such an essential part of one's overall happiness, especially after all materialistic needs are met, we cannot help but say that the fate of His Royal Highness leaves much to be desired.

Of course, it is unfair to lay all the blame on his forehead. In fact, his trademark protruding ears also share some of the responsibility. While thick, fleshy, and fairly long, his ears conspicuously protrude forward from the top. Chinese physiognomy takes this to indicate emotional trouble, a physically unstable life characterized by frequent travel or changes in career, and a personality that likes to move around a lot, coupled with charm and humor. No doubt, the ears also contribute to his unhappy emotional and marital life.

If you take a closer look at his ears, you will notice that they contain thick earlobes and prominent inner circles. The thick earlobes have a lot to do with his royal background, and the prominent inner circles signify that this is an ambitious person who cares much more about the throne than sexual pleasure. However, he seems to have an arduous uphill battle to fight before he can ascend to the throne, mostly due to his weak chin.

永美命

Chapter 10

Eyebrows

Eyebrows are one of the most outstanding features of the face due to their distinctive color. They are the location of the Siblings Palaces and are regarded as the protectors of the eyes. Besides providing us information about our brothers and sisters, eyebrows also indicate one's mental ability, artistic tastes, literary talents and, particularly, one's personality.

Several generalizations can be made regarding the physiognomic significance of eyebrows by analyzing the following qualities: thickness, length, orderliness, and position. These interpretations generally apply to both men and women.

Thickness: Generally speaking, thick eyebrows are preferable to thin ones in that thick eyebrows symbolize a greater degree of physical courage, loyalty, uprightness, frankness, sportsmanship, and sexuality. Typically, such a person is brave, ready to fight, takes risks, and stands up for what he or she believes to be right. No wonder many great soldiers in history possess bushy eyebrows. Examples include Lin Biao, Zhu De (the first of the ten marshals of the Communist China), Nagumo (a World War II admiral), former Soviet leader Leonid Brezhnev, and Ayatollah Khomeini of Iran.

On the negative side, people with thick eyebrows are often short-tempered and impatient, coupled with a strong personality that almost borders on dictatorship. Courageous and efficient at work, people with thick eyebrows have a natural tendency to resort to physical violence whenever confronted or insulted. In fact, they are more sensitive to threats posed to them, be it physical or verbal, and have a strong urge to right the wrong done to them or their friends. They want to be in a winning situation and commanding position, either in society or in the family.

People with thin eyebrows are more shrewd, timid, conservative, and sexually weak. They do not allow others to enter their mind easily. The Chinese speak of such people as having "great walls" guarding their mind and intentions. Physically, they are more vulnerable to disease than those with thick eyebrows.

Length: Long eyebrows, meaning wider than the eyes, are considered auspicious. Those with such eyebrows tend to be more outgoing and have greater literary and artistic tastes than those with short eyebrows. Long eyebrows are indicate a long life.

People with short eyebrows are often found to be lonely, shy, rude, and uninterested in schooling. They prefer to keep their problems to themselves rather than sharing them with others. However, short, thick, and bushy eyebrows are suggestive of extraordinary courage and high military position. In fact, many military leaders have short eyebrows such as Zhu De.

The eyebrows are also the location of the Sibling Palaces, which indicate the number of siblings one will have. It is the length of the eyebrows that provides us this information: those with longer eyebrows tend to have more brothers and sisters than their counterparts with short eyebrows. The Sibling Palaces or eyebrows also reveal the relationship among the siblings. These relationships are considered an important element in one's fate, because traditional Chinese culture is very family-oriented. Those with long eyebrows usually have more brothers and sisters than those with short eyebrows and they enjoy a greater degree of affection with them. Chinese face divination takes the length of the eyebrow as a measure of the length of friendship. This is true for both genders.

Order: Chinese physiognomy tells us that if the eyebrows lie in an orderly, graceful manner, and turn upward slightly, then the person has a friendly nature. This person will also be close to his brothers and sisters and they will all have good careers.

If the eyebrows look chaotic or discontinued in places (bare spots), that person's brothers and sisters will behave more like strangers, or even worse. Such siblings cannot be counted on in times of need.

Position: The position of the eyebrows in regard to the eyes is another important quality. The fathers of face reading hold that the closer the eyebrows are to the eyes, the more impatient, narrow-minded, and intolerant will the person be. Eyebrows that are pressing on the eyes indicate one who is easily offended and revengeful, even against the most minor offenses. This personality makes one a hard companion, and can cause serious trouble for the person around the age of thirty, such as a major physical injury or legal problems.

By contrast, those with high-set eyebrows, those that lie farther above the eyes, are more tolerant of others, patient, generous, and easy-going. They forgive and forget. Their interpersonal skills are good, and they have an easy time making and keeping friends.

Occasionally, there are people who have eyebrows set at different levels, where one eyebrow is higher than the other. This interesting phenomenon suggests that the person has a stepparent and/or stepsiblings. Such asymmetrical eyebrows typically mean that brothers and sisters come from different parents. It can also indicate moodiness or changing emotions.

Other qualities to look for in eyebrows are whether they are shiny or dull, curved or straight.

To sum up, ideal eyebrows are shiny, orderly, longer than the eyes, and curve upward.

On the following pages is a list of specific eyebrow types and their fate interpretations.

Figure 10.1: Sword eyebrows

Figure 10.2: Knife eyebrows

Sword Eyebrows

Sword eyebrows are thick, shiny, long, orderly and graceful; typically handsome and eye-catching when found in a male's face. (See Figure 10.1.) Those with sword eyebrows are courageous, energetic, decisive, farsighted, and have a strong inclination toward leadership. Though ambitious and daring, people with such eyebrows are not selfish, at least not in a petty way. They tend to be very active in social affairs, and chances are great that such people will make a name for themselves early in life. They are capable of instilling faith and optimism into a group of followers. Fathers of face reading believed these people could be strong assistants to their emperors. They are bound to have good luck with honor and power.

Knife Eyebrows

These eyebrows take the shape of a knife with the inner ends of the eyebrows resembling the handle of a knife and the outer ends resembling the knife blade. (See Figure 10.2.) This kind of eyebrow tends to belong to cruel and decisive people who won't bat an eyelid in killing their enemies. Many rebel leaders and warlords possess such eyebrows. Chiang Kai-shek and Iran's Ayatollah Khomeini are good examples.

Devil's Eyebrows

This type of eyebrow is bushy and chaotic, with the hairs sticking out in all directions. (See Figure 10.3, page 91.) Devil's eyebrows suggest a very selfish, cruel, corrupted, and vicious character who is suspicious,

Figure 10.3: Devil's eyebrows

Figure 10.4: Broom eyebrows

especially when the eyebrows are pressing on the eyes (close set). Plus, they are liable to mental disorders, such as paranoia.

Broom Eyebrows

Broom eyebrows are very thick and relatively short. (See Figure 10.4.) Owners of such eyebrows are decisive, aggressive, and sanguine. They fit best for a military career or other fields in which physical courage and strong hands are indispensable to career success. Although such people can suddenly rise to power, wealth, and fame, their ending is usually not very good, with a great chance of death as sudden and mysterious as their rise to power and wealth.

Character "One" Eyebrows

These eyebrows resemble the Chinese character for the number one. (See Figure 10.5, page 92.) Owners of such eyebrows belong to those who have powerful, friendly brothers and beautiful, devoted wives. They are themselves friendly, upright, and bright, and will have a happy family and enjoy honor and prosperity.

Character "Eight" Eyebrows

These eyebrows resemble the Chinese character for the number eight when viewed together. (See Figure 10.6, page 92.) Chinese physiognomy warns of the selfish, mean, and vengeful nature of those who possess such eyebrows. Although bright and smart, these people are typically preoccupied

Figure 10.5: Character "One" eyebrows

Figure 10.6: Character "Eight" eyebrows

with stepping on other people's toes for their own gain and promotion. They have great worldly desires, and they do not care about what means they employ in achieving their goals. However, if their eyes look kind and gentle, the damage they do to others will be greatly reduced.

Short-thick Eyebrows

At first glance, these eyebrows are not all that different from broom eyebrows, but while both are shiny and bushy, short-thick eyebrows are more orderly and slightly curve up at the ends. (See Figure 10.7, page 93.) People with such eyebrows are hardworking, courageous, but hot-tempered and impatient. They are often blessed with longevity and a big family; this is partly because the thickness of the eyebrows suggests sexual vitality, which is vital to

increasing the family size. Since short-thick eyebrows are more graceful than broom eyebrows, these people usually have greater artistic talents or tastes. They can also succeed in both military and literary fields.

Crescent Eyebrows

These eyebrows are so named because they look like a crescent moon: curved, delicate, and graceful. (See Figure 10.8, page 93.) Since the moon is the female image of gentleness and symbolizes art and literature, those owning such eyebrows are said to be gentle, sensitive, bright, and gifted with artistic and literary talents. Many of them are sensualists and tend to lead an open, free life. They may not have many brothers and sisters, but the ones they have are friendly and affectionate. On the minus side, these people are often sentimental,

Figure 10.7: Short-thick eyebrows

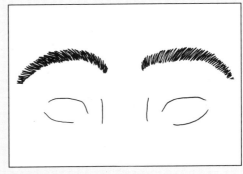

Figure 10.8: Crescent eyebrows

given to depression and worry, and lack the tenacity to see their ideas successfully implemented to the end.

High-set Eyebrows

Some people have their eyebrows set high on their forehead, far away from the eyes. (See Figure 10.9, page 94.) Such eyebrows indicate that their owners are far-sighted, with a great chance of becoming political leaders. They must have considerable social positions to ensure that their livelihoods are sustained throughout life. These people are also very demanding in terms of privacy; they want to keep their private life private. Even as leaders, they will try to shy away from the media and public appearances as much as they can.

Willow Eyebrows

These eyebrows are very long, slightly curved, and very graceful, like the leaves of a willow tree. (See Figure 10.10, page 94.) Willow is a symbol of sentimentality, lasting friendship, and literary talent in China. Therefore, owners of willow eyebrows are considered intelligent, friendly, sentimental, romantic, and graceful. They often excel in the arts and literature. In fact, many famous poets and authors and are found to have such eyebrows. Li Bai, one of the greatest Chinese poets, was said to have a pair of willow eyebrows. Lin Shu, a famous Chinese author and translator at the turn of the century, also possessed such a pair of eyebrows.

Those with willow eyebrows also have a strong appetite for both knowledge and the

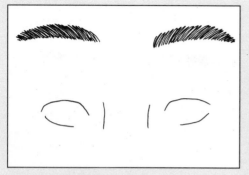

Figure 10.9: High-set eyebrows

Figure 10.10: Willow eyebrows

Figure 10.11: Yin-Yang eyebrows

Figure 10.12: Triangular eyebrows

opposite sex, and can enjoy a long life. Unfortunately, marriage usually comes late in life, and family life tends not to be very satisfactory. These people typically have better relationships with friends than with family members.

Yin-Yang Eyebrows

These eyebrows are so called because they possess opposite characteristics, just like yin and yang are opposites. For instance, one eyebrow may be thick but the other is thin; one may be high while the other is low; or one is shiny but the other dim, etc.

Figure 10.13: Joined eyebrows

(See Figure 10.11, page 94.) These asymmetrical eyebrows suggest divorce or separation on the part of parents, stepbrothers or stepsisters, fluctuation in family life, and a calculating mind skillful at playing politics. Indeed, many owners of such eyebrows end up becoming brilliant politicians or military leaders. For instance, Yang Shankun, the late president of China, possessed yin-yang eyebrows.

Triangular Eyebrows

Resembling a triangular shape, these eyebrows belong to people who are capable of great courage and decision-making, often coupled with foresight and strong intuition. (See Figure 10.12, page 94.) If the nose is also good, owners of such eyebrows stand a great chance of becoming famous generals

or politicians, especially during times of war. On the downside, they are very suspicious, selfish, and cruel, especially when the eyes are also triangular shaped.

Joined Eyebrows

These eyebrows actually meet, looking like one big eyebrow across the forehead. (See Figure 10.13.) Such eyebrows indicate a worrying nature, a hard childhood, poor family background, and great misfortune—often in the form of a prison sentence before the age of thirty.

Indeed, owners of such eyebrows have little to boast of and take advantage of family help. They are often frustrated, and have to double their efforts in order to achieve the same level of success as others. In fact, quite a few famous world politicians are born with such eyebrows.

A lot of their future depends on whether the nose is good or not. If the nose is auspicious, as in the cases of Joseph Stalin and Nelson Mandela, they will survive early misfortune and emerge as powerful leaders.

This seems to confirm the famous statement made by Mencius two thousand years ago, which should give some consolation to those born with joined eyebrows: "If Heaven has a great mandate for someone, it will first torture him in various ways while he is young: deprive him of his due food and

	Thickness	Length	Order	Position
Auspicious	thick	long	smooth orderly	high above eyes
Inauspicious	thin	short	chaotic	close to eyes

Table 10.1: Summary of criteria for eyebrows

clothing, work him hard physically and mentally, with the course of events running counter to his desire. All these devices have one purpose, and that is to train him in his willpower, make him much more patient and tenacious than ordinary people, and add greatly to his ability so that he can achieve great deeds in the future."

Chapter 11

Eyes

The eyes are referred to as the "window of one's mind" in Chinese culture. So long as the window is open, masters of face reading will always be able to see into the other's mind. In this sense, eyes are the single most important feature in face reading, especially when you want to establish a close relationship with the person being read, be it business, political, or marital. In fact, no other part of the face tells more about a person's personality than the eyes.

According to the fathers of Chinese face reading, the eyes are so important that if the eyes are good but none of the other features are, the person will still be intelligent and have good luck sooner or later. If the other features are good while the eyes are bad (in a physiognomic sense), the person will not be very successful no matter how good the family background is.

To analyze these important "windows," the criteria to look at are size, eye contact, focus, and color. These characteristics apply to both genders, with some exceptions for women.

Size: For instance, those with large eyes have strong emotions and artistic gifts. However, they are often not careful enough with monetary matters. Those with small eyes are cautious people. They like to think in a comprehensive way when making decisions, weighing the pros and cons over and over again before taking any action. Large eyes are not necessarily better than small ones; they are just different in terms of personality.

Eye contact: The way in which a person's eyes make contact with another person's eyes reveals information about one's personality. If one always looks above the other's head, this must be a proud and arrogant person. If one always looks downward, then they must be timid, exercising unusual caution and often worried. In similar token, if one keeps casting glances about in an uneasy way, rather than confronting the other's eyes, the person is bound to harbor some ulterior motives. Either the person is

trying to steal something or intends harm on someone sexually.

Similarly, if one dares not look straight into the other's eyes while facing each other, one must have a bad conscience, feels guilty, or has done something wrong to others. Such a person can hardly be considered upright and trustworthy. If it's a woman, she tends to be of loose character with no sense of fidelity.

If eye contact is always direct, straight, powerful, and penetrating, the person must be bright and brave, with a clean conscience. The person has a high opinion of himself but does not think much of others.

Gaze or focus: The manner in which a person gazes or focuses indicates more about their luck than their personality. If a person has trouble focusing or is constantly looking at other things, such a person does not have self-confidence, nor does the person have definite objectives or goals. Therefore, such a person will not travel very far in life. On the other hand, if the gaze is focused and penetrating, the person will be logical, with clear objectives, be determined in action, and farsighted in thinking. Such a person can be expected to be loyal and stable in emotion and career, and achieve a lot in life.

Color: Color is of vital importance in the divination of the eyes. Auspicious eyes must have dark pupils surrounded by silvery white areas ("whites of the eyes"). Such eyes suggest intelligence, nobility, longevity, and authority.

On the contrary, if the white areas are yellow, red, or largely white, the eyes are inauspicious. Such a person must be mean in character, short-tempered, timid, dull, and potentially dangerous to others. If the eyes are full of red lines, several possibilities exist: the person either has or will be involved in a lawsuit, an accident, a fight with others, or a violent and sudden death away from home. (Generally, these colors are universal for all ethnic groups.)

There are also some gender differences in judging the eyes. Traditionally, for a male, the gaze should be powerful and penetrating, whereas for a female it should be focused but gentle. Gentleness is the assumed character of the fairer sex, and it applies to their facial features as well. It is also said that if a woman's eyes often look misty or watery, chances are she is either too sexy for her own good, with strong temporal desires, or she will bring misfortune and even a violent death to her husband.

Besides the eye itself, the two small areas right beneath the eyes are also worthy of study. These small areas are known as the Children's Palaces or "sleeping silkworms." They are exclusively related to one's children, indicating the number of offspring, their health, fortune, as well as one's relationship with them. Round, full,

solid, and bright, "sleeping silkworms" suggest that one is destined to have intelligent, healthy, and filial children. It is suggested that if the left sleeping silkworm is solid and bright, one will have two good children. If the right sleeping silkworm is solid, full, and bright, one will have three good children. If both sleeping silkworms are round, full, solid, and bright, one will have at least five children who are intelligent, healthy, and have good careers.

On the other hand, if these areas are sunken, dark, or marred by moles or lines, one runs the risk of having children who are in poor health or in prison. They also indicate that either one is forced to separate from their children or their relationship with their children is strained.

In summary, good eyes are bright, sharp, and large, curving upward. Bad eyes are small, dim, drunken, unfocused, and slant downward.

As pointed out earlier, Chinese face divination derives a lot of its theory and insight from the animal world. This is perhaps most manifested in the classification and characterization of human eyes. Personally, I have been advised by my teachers to spend a lot of time at the zoo studying the habits, mannerisms, and faces of different animals.

The following pages list the various types of eyes and their characteristics.

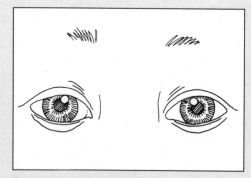

Figure 11.1: Dragon eyes

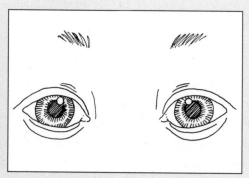

Figure 11.2: Phoenix eyes

Dragon Eyes

The mighty and magnificent dragon of mythical origin never ceases to trigger the imagination of Chinese face readers. In China, the dragon symbolizes supreme nobility, power, authority, and good luck. All of the following qualities are believed to exist in those who possess dragon eyes: creativity, vitality, foresight, power, and authority—the most essential traits underlying a successful leadership. No wonder such eyes can only be found in top leaders.

Dragon eyes are large with round, double lids and well-curved lower rims slanting upward. (See Figure 11.1.) The black pupils in these eyes are very large, occupying more than two-thirds of the whole eye area. Dragon eyes are powerful yet charming, graceful, shiny and penetrating; penetrating in the sense that they seem to look directly into the other's mind. Their very gaze inspires confidence and respect. Therefore, dragon eyes are among the most desirable types of eyes.

Phoenix Eyes

Phoenix eyes are the female counterpart to dragon eyes. Equally legendary and mythical, the phoenix represents female power and authority, culminated in the position of a queen.

Phoenix eyes are very large, bright, charming, and graceful, decorated with round, double lids and well-curved upper rims. (See Figure 11.2.) Typically, the pupils are also very large, occupying more than two-thirds of the whole eye. Owners of such eyes, male or female, will be kind and noble, and enjoy wealth, fame, love, and power.

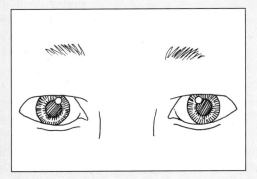

Figure 11.3: Tiger eyes

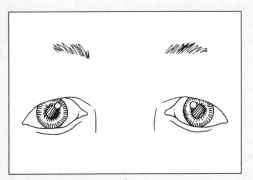

Figure 11.4: Fox eyes

Tiger Eyes

The outstanding characteristic of tiger eyes is their rectangular shape. They seem to have angles at all four corners, so they strike people as more rectangular than round. (See Figure 11.3.) In traditional Chinese culture, the tiger symbolizes power, courage, wealth, vitality, and good luck. Therefore, owners of tiger eyes are judged to be brave, farsighted, entrepreneurial, energetic, and creative. They are born to be leaders and can hardly conform to the established status quo. In fact, many political and military leaders in transitional ages such as the age in which one dynasty is to be replaced by another, possessed such eyes. Throughout their lives, they do not have to worry about their livelihood, although their mind is hardly preoccupied with personal wealth.

One way or the other, money will come to them without their even seeking it.

It is said that owners of tiger eyes are somewhat restless and rebellious. This is to be expected, given the nature of the tiger. However, once they are committed to a project, everything, including eating and sleeping, will have to take second place in pursuit of success. Also, tiger eyes have very strong egos. When their ego is hurt, money and power mean little to them. This is the key to maintaining a good working relationship or friendship with them.

Fox Eyes

Angular, small, and slanting downward, fox eyes signify a natural cunning and avarice on the part of their owners. (See Figure 11.4.) People with such eyes are generally

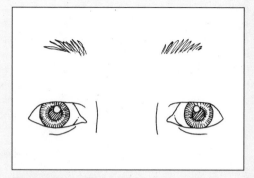

Figure 11.5: Cat eyes

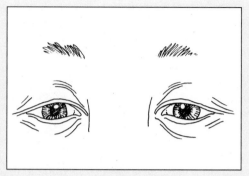

Figure 11.6: Snake eyes

greedy, shrewd, or too clever. Their relationships with colleagues are usually tense, especially after a period of close work. Their very shrewdness could make them appear to be good in interpersonal skills before their true intentions are revealed.

Cat Eyes

Cat eyes are somewhat similar to tiger eyes but shorter. Both are shiny and powerful with corners and a penetrating gaze. (See Figure 11.5.) This similarity is well understood, for in China, the cat is regarded as a small tiger, so the cat possesses some of the qualities of its larger relative, albeit in a lesser magnitude.

Those with cat eyes are believed to be on guard all the time, sensitive and alert to external threats. However, they do not have as strong an ego as the owners of tiger

eyes, and are not so easily provoked. They are also blessed with good luck, power, and fame, although they can hardly be top leaders themselves; they seem to best fit into the position of second or third. This is because there are just too many more powerful animals than cats in nature.

Snake Eyes

Snake eyes are small, blue (by Chinese standards), and somewhat swollen. (See Figure 11.6.) The Chinese refer to those with wicked and malicious intentions as having "a heart of a snake." This is exactly what snake eyes tell about their owners. Merciless, calculating, revengeful, always thinking of taking advantage of others or hurting others, owners of snake eyes are good at espionage. In ordinary life, however, these are people to be kept at a respect-

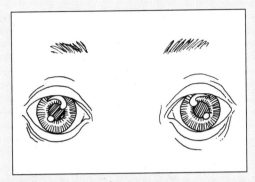

Figure 11.7: Monkey eyes

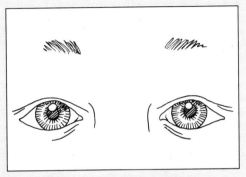

Figure 11.8: Mandarin duck eyes

ful distance. Their smiles should be taken as venom.

Monkey Eyes

Monkey eyes are shiny, round, slightly protruding and look as if they are always on the move. (See Figure 11.7.) They project the impression of intelligence and alertness. Just like the innovative, flexible, and often mischievous monkey, owners of such eyes are highly intelligent, with a strong memory and intuition. They are calculating, suspicious, shrewd, impatient, lecherous, revengeful, and extremely adroit in self-preservation. They are vulnerable to temptations, sexual temptations in particular. At times, they can be mischievous, but always in a disarmingly pleasant way.

Mandarin Duck Eyes

These eyes are long with large pupils. (See Figure 11.8.) Fathers of face divination hold that those with Mandarin duck eyes are lucky in money, gifted with super intelligence, and preoccupied with sex and power. To be successful in a career, however, they have to possess a good nose and forehead as well. Otherwise, they will have a hard time achieving success.

Triangular Eyes

As the term implies, triangular eyes have a clear triangular shape. (See Figure 11.9, page 104.) Owners of such eyes are calculating, suspicious, cruel, and cunning. These are very smart people, but they are not to be trusted because they are more bright than upright. In the worst case, owners of such

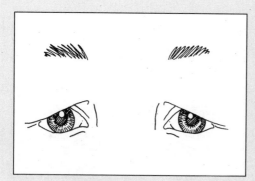

Figure 11.9: Triangular eyes

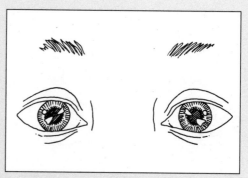

Figure 11.10: Bear eyes

eyes will not hesitate to stab others in the back if they see fit to do so. Actually, quite a few successful politicians, generals, and merchants have such eyes. To them, the ends justifies the means.

Bear Eyes

Bear eyes are dull and somewhat protruded, with a large white area and small pupils. (See Figure 11.10.) The light from the eyes seems to shatter around as if there is no focal point of attention. Owners of bear eyes are usually lacking in intelligence, lazy but daring, with the tendency to commit crimes. Oftentimes, they have trouble concentrating on what they are doing, and feel at a loss as to what they should do. At the urging of their own emotions or another's persuasion, they can overreact to a situation and cause damage to themselves or others.

Wolf Eyes

Wolf eyes are long, bright, fiercely penetrating, and they slant slightly downward at the outer corners, with red lines. (See Figure 11.11, page 105.) The color of the pupils are a mixture of blue and white, projecting a desire to kill and devour. At night, wolf eyes look unusually bright. Owners of such eyes are very cruel, fierce, revengeful, and malicious, with an unsatisfied appetite for power and control. If their eyes are also long, they are bound to hold high social positions. However, they are often subject to violent and sudden death. Their tempers are short, and their minds narrow. Indeed, they delight in seeing others suffer. They often turn out to be arch criminals, war mongers, or gang leaders. It is said that the notorious premier Qin Kui of the Southern Song Dynasty possessed a pair of wolf eyes.

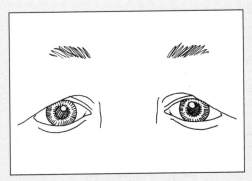

Figure 11.11: Wolf eyes

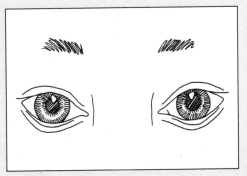

Figure 11.12: Crane eyes

Qin Kui betrayed his own country, collaborated with the enemy, and murdered the national hero Marshal Yue Fei and his eldest son.

Crane Eyes

Crane eyes have dark pupils and are beautifully curved, coupled with double eyelids. (See Figure 11.12.) Possessors of such eyes have a strong artistic taste, and are capable of brilliant civil careers, either as scientists, doctors, authors, or professors. They have a natural thirst for truth and knowledge, and are capable of working hard to acquire the skills needed to advance their careers.

Lion Eyes

Lion eyes are long with a stable and penetrating gaze. Such eyes look imposing, some-

what fearful to others without the person being angry. (See Figure 11.13, page 106.) Such eyes suggest wealth, intelligence, determination, presence of mind, social position, and courage on the part of their owners. Those with lion eyes are best suited for executive careers, either in business, politics, or the military. They are no-nonsense types of people, working hard and demanding the same from subordinates.

Elephant Eyes

Elephant eyes are long, bright, full, and gracefully curved, with big and impressive pupils. (See Figure 11.14, page 106) Chinese physiognomy regards owners of such eyes as well-to-do, honorable, kind-hearted, and healthy. To them, wealth comes slowly but steadily as a reward for their consistent effort and faithful services.

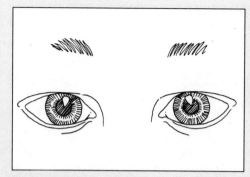

Figure 11.13: Lion eyes

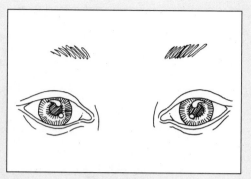

Figure 11.14: Elephant eyes

Horse Eyes

Horse eyes are large, round, and slightly protruding, with double eyelids and beautifully curved rims. (See Figure 11.15, page 107.) Such eyes reveal that their owners are intelligent, quick-witted, frank, hard-working, and gifted with literary and artistic taste. On the down side, owners of such eyes usually have short tempers. Calling a spade a spade, they do not know how to hide their true feelings. For this, they may open themselves to misunderstandings, but eventually, their intelligence and good intentions will be appreciated by others, though not without a price.

Deer Eyes

Deer eyes are very similar to horse eyes. The main difference lies in that deer eyes are smaller. (See Figure 11.16, page 107.) These

eyes belong to people who are friendly, kind-hearted, intelligent, and persistent but often impatient. They are very sensitive to any danger around them, and are quick to point it out to their friends. This very sensitivity to potentially evil forces makes them rather restless at heart, although their appearance may suggest a different story. Fathers of face reading also note that these are people whose physical courage is equaled by their moral courage. They are also stable forces for others in times of emergency.

Cow Eyes

Cow eyes strike people as steady, gentle, decisive, and trustworthy. They are not typically large, but have big pupils with a stable gaze. (See Figure 11.17, page 107.) Cow eyes indicate a hard working, reliable, patient, and courageous person. These peo-

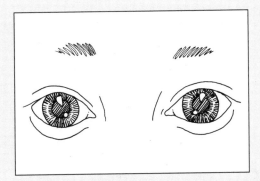

Figure 11.15: Horse eyes

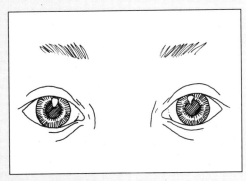

Figure 11.16: Deer eyes

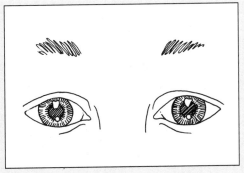

Figure 11.17: Cow eyes

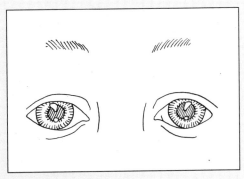

Figure 11.18: Ram eyes

ple won't let you down nor will they desert you in times of need if they consider you to be a friend. Their working style is slow but steady, and their thinking is very logical and methodological. They make good scientists, doctors, and spouses.

Ram Eyes

Ram eyes are similar to cow eyes but are smaller and more graceful, with double eyelids and beautifully curved. (See Figure 11.18, page 107.) The pupils are fully surrounded on all sides by white areas. People born with ram eyes are timid, lecherous, and fond of comfort. Although intelligent

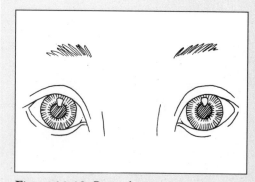

Figure 11.19: Peacock eyes

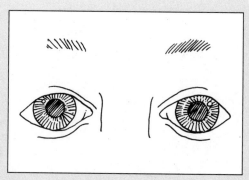

Figure 11.20: Pig eyes

and gifted, they often lack the courage and diligence to carry out their bright ideas. They have a tendency to dissipate their limited energy for the sake of temporal pleasures; many could be considered womanizers. This is one of the reasons why ram-eyed people often have a short life. Unless supported by a strong nose and chin, their success in a career will be substantially limited.

Peacock Eyes

Peacock eyes are very round. (See Figure 11.19.) They reflect the vicissitude in the fortune of their owners. Typically, their marital life is subject to some kind of misfortune: either their spouses die early or they divorce. Money and position are mixed blessings for them, because many

people are jealous of them and try to undermine their position. Those with peacock eyes usually do not have many friends, but for those they do have, peacock eyes owners can be good friends who are ready to make great sacrifices for them.

Pig Eyes

Pig eyes are small and dull, with a vague look. (See Figure 11.20.) Owners of such eyes are usually dull, conservative, short-sighted, and often harbor ulterior motives to try to take advantage of others. They are not likely to hold leadership positions, but are best suited to detailed work. In addition, their life span is usually short, living no more than sixty years.

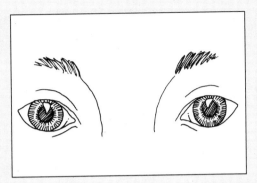

Figure 11.21: Wide-set eyes

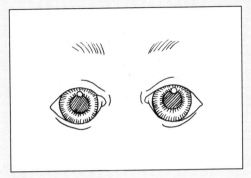

Figure 11.22: Close-set eyes

Wide-set Eyes

Eyes set far apart suggest that their owners are energetic, optimistic, farsighted, and open-minded. (See Figure 11.21.) They seem to have endless energy, and are capable of hard work for long periods. Their very presence serves to inspire confidence and an air of victory. They take things easy, knowing that there is always tomorrow. They are find it easy to forgive others as well as themselves. This personality makes them welcome colleagues (if you do not want to rush a project) and enables them to live longer than others. On the negative side, such people are sometimes given to daydreaming.

Close-set Eyes

If the distance between the eyes is no wider that a finger, then such eyes are considered closely set against each other. People with eyes set close together are more dogmatic, pessimistic, and narrow-minded. (See Figure 11.22.) They tend to go by the book, and can be very good clerks and secretaries. They have a hard time taking a long-term view of life, being preoccupied with current affairs. They also find it difficult to forgive and forget. If you wrong them, even unintentionally, they will most likely remember it for a long time. Oftentimes, their health is not good, and they feel lacking in energy and drive for strategic planning for their own life.

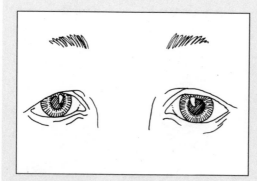

Figure 11.23: Yin-yang eyes

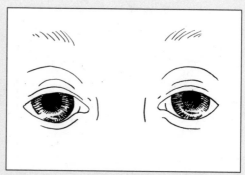

Figure 11.24: Drunken eyes

Yin-Yang Eyes

These eyes are not the same in size. (See Figure 11.23.) Owners of such eyes are naturally smart and calculating, gifted in monetary affairs, and have a good chance to become successful business people. In fact, many wealthy people are found to have such eyes. These people are very suspicious and alert and do not make friends easily. Their fortune is subject to ups and downs, especially during middle age.

Fathers of face reading regard people with eyes of distinctively different sizes as farsighted, because the smaller eye is used to look at the earth and the larger eye is used to observe the heaven. Not surprisingly, many people with yin-yang eyes are found in high social positions. However, such a pair of eyes is an indication of a short life, unless the owner has long ears and a round chin, where they then can live past the age of eighty.

Drunken Eyes

Such eyes look like the person is drunk, projecting a vague look lacking focus. (See Figure 11.24.) Drunken eyes are a sign of love for sex, irresponsibility, unhappy marriage, and possible sudden death in middle age. Success in a career is hard to come by, and money acquired will be lost eventually.

Peach Blossom Eyes

These eyes are very beautiful, bright, and expressive, as if "floating like water and charming like peach flowers." (See Figure 11.25, page 111.) Owners of such eyes must

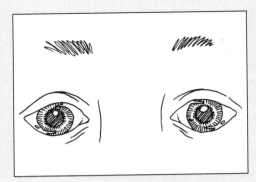

Figure 11.25: Peach blossom eyes

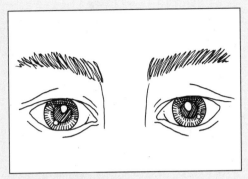

Figure 11.26: Powerful eyes

be very lucky in love, typically having numerous affairs throughout their lives. They are very attractive to the opposite sex. They have little sense of loyalty in terms of relationships, and are constantly looking for new acquaintances. Indeed, their sexual appetite never seems to know its limit. Such characteristics indicate that they are bound to run into a marriage crisis. They do not seem to care about it, though; to them, life is a never-ending search for new conquests. Many famous Chinese actors, actresses, business people, and politicians are found to possess such eyes.

Powerful Eyes

These eyes are majestic, penetrating, and fierce enough to subdue one's enemy by their very gaze (See Figure 11.26.) People with such eyes project a strong sense of power and command immediate respect and fear without resorting to anger. They can hold great power and authority, especially military power. They are very likely to become famous or notorious in times of war or turbulence, born leaders in the military.

	Size	Contact	Gaze	Color
Auspicious	large	direct	focused, penetrating	large, dark pupils, silvery whites
Inauspicious	small	indirect	indirect, scattered	small pupils, yellow or red whites, red lines

Table 11.1: Summary of criteria for eyes

Summary Reading #3: Eyebrows and Eyes

Test your knowledge on chapters 10 and 11. Look at the photo of the popular world figure on the following page and try to read his face, specifically analyzing his eyebrows and eyes. Then see how closely your analysis matches the author's interpretation.

Albert Einstein, most famous for his discovery of the theory of relativity, was a mathematician, physicist, philosopher, physician, and musician.

AP Photo

Albert Einstein

Eyebrows: _____

_____

_____

_____

_____

Eyes: _____

_____

_____

_____

_____

Author's interpretation: It is a Chinese physiognomic belief that great men must have great eyes. As we look into the eyes of Einstein, we are once more convinced of this ancient Chinese wisdom.

Einstein's eyes were large, graceful, shiny, penetrating, and powerful—all auspicious signs. In Chinese physiognomy, they are also referred to as "schools," signifying the knowledge and intelligence one possesses. It is little wonder that such a pair of eyes were found in the face of this great genius, scholar, and Nobel Prize winner. His imaginative and intuitive powers and his insight into human knowledge were astonishingly profound.

In fact, his excellent eyes signified not only his superb intelligence, but also his outstanding social position and international fame. The graceful contour of his eyes, the large pupils, and the powerful but gentle light emanating from them, all argued strongly for a noble position in a civil instead of a military field. Also indicated was his kind heart, which reached out to all the world.

On top of his eyes were a pair of thick but curving eyebrows, which stood out in clear profile and cut as conspicuous a figure as his eyes did. The very thickness of his eyebrows spoke loudly for his moral courage and strong personality as a leader in the cutting edge of science. However, if these eyebrows were merely thick but not curving and graceful, Einstein might have ended up as a general instead of a leading scholar.

Nonetheless, the strong and occasionally hot temper of this giant was physiognomically detectable by his penetrating eyes. Indeed, he could sometimes be impatient.

Separated from but closely related to the quality of his eyebrows was the space between them—the Life Palace. Notice how spacious and protruding his Life Palace was. It ensured that this was a person who would have a bright future, coupled with an extraordinarily strong life force to see him through all the ordeals in his life. The fact that Einstein escaped unscathed from the Nazi reign in his early years and emerged as one of the greatest personalities of our century was no mere coincidence. His extraordinary eyes and eyebrows clearly showed the cause and effect of fate working in his life.

Chapter 12

福 Nose

According to the Three Portions system, the nose is the "human" portion of the face, lying between heaven (forehead) and earth (chin). The nose is a very important object in the reading of a face, for it stands for many things in one's life.

First of all, the nose governs the fate of your middle age. It is also the location where your wealth and health are assessed—the Wealth Palace and the Health Palace. No wonder fathers of face divination attached so great an importance to this single feature. They hold that unless the nose is above average in quality, one cannot hope to climb very high in social position and material wealth, no matter how good the other features may be.

The nose also stands for one's spouse. For a female, it is called "the husband star," while for a male it is known as "the wife star." The nose determines to a great extent whether or not one can find a good spouse, whether marital life will be happy, and if your spouse will be attractive.

It is not hard to understand why the quality of nose matters so much for the happiness of marriage. Since the nose is where one's Wealth Palace is located, it means first and foremost one's financial ability. This ability seems to weigh more heavily than most other factors when coming to marriage, since, too often, money can speak louder than most other things when it comes to choosing a mate. Generally, a financially strong man or woman has a better chance of marrying someone of their choosing than a financially weak person.

Besides the clues that a nose can provide regarding one's social position, financial strength, and marital life, the nose is also the symbol of life energy. This energy manifests itself in health status, sexuality, ability to work long hours on the run, and efficiency of work.

Finally, the nose helps reveal one's intentions and personality. For instance, if the nose is slanted, biased, or leaning toward one side, this reveals that the person is not honest. Most likely, he or she harbors some ill motives against others, although not all the time or against all people. In contrast, if the nose is straight, balanced, and unbiased, the person is more likely to have good intentions.

The criteria to look at in a nose are the nose bridge and the nose tip and wings. The nose bridge is the upper, bony part of the nose. The nose tip is self-explanatory while the wings refer to the "bumps" on either side of the nose tip or the nostrils. The characteristics and meanings generally apply to both men and women.

Nose bridge: It is an ancient Chinese belief that to hold a high social position, one must have a nose with a high and straight bridge. The truth of this belief can be easily verified just by observing the noses of dignitaries. Margaret Thatcher, John F. Kennedy, Prince Charles of Wales, Princess Diana, Albert Einstein, Bill Clinton, Ronald Reagan, Japan's Crown Prince Naruhito, and Crown Princess Owada Masako are all good examples.

For a man, the higher and straighter the nose bridge (and the fuller and bigger the nose tip and wings), the prettier and more helpful his wife will be. In other words, he will be lucky in his relationships and happy in marriage, if he chooses to get married. He does not have to spend a lot of time trying to find and please a girlfriend; women cannot seem to resist his appeal.

A high and straight nose also signifies a strong life energy and a more positive attitude towards life. Generally speaking, those with a high nose bridge are more aggressive, ambitious, outgoing, and efficient at work.

A nose with a low bridge, a crooked bridge, or one with bumps will greatly hinder one's career, a political career in particular. A crooked nose also signifies a crooked mind. Such a nose indicates a high potential for extramarital affairs. It even predicts the same thing for one's spouse.

A bumpy, crooked, or low nose signifies frustration and failure in marriage and relationships. Several things may happen as a result: either the spouse is in poor health; has a temper and unfriendly personality; is unattractive or unappealing in appearance; will divorce, often more than once; or the spouse will die early in life, leaving the widower grieving for the rest of his or her life. One way or the other, one's relational and marital life will leave much to be desired.

While not all people with a straight nose are upright and fair, those with a crooked or slanted nose are likely to be crooked and slanted in their thinking and dealings with others. They tend to harbor ulterior motives, to take advantage of others, or think of underhanded ways to advance their career or benefit their families. They have a strong tendency for vengeance. These are the people who have a very long memory and find it hard to forgive and forget when offended. Masters of face reading advise one to carefully watch out for such people if one happens to work or live with them. This does not necessarily mean that they are not good people; they are not malicious all the time. Their malice is most likely vented against their enemies. They are also likely to suffer from ill health for at least a certain part of their lives.

If a nose is small in the proportion of the entire face, or if it is short by the same measurement, or if it has a very low bridge, such a nose indicates lack of life energy and a pessimistic attitude towards life.

Nose tip and wings: While the height of the nose can tell about one's social position, the size of the nose tip and its two wings reveal the secret of one's financial strength. Those with a big, round nose tip and full, fleshy nose wings, and invisible nostrils are destined to possess financial wealth. Such a nose is the best insurance against poverty and financial insecurity in life. Examples of this kind of nose can be found in the faces of former English prime minister Margaret Thatcher, Queen Elizabeth II, former U. S. presidents Ronald Reagan and John F.

Kennedy, Mao Tse-tung, and Deng Xiao-ping.

A pointed nose tip with thin wings and visible nostrils is a sure sign of financial difficulty. If you happen to possess such a nose, you'd better steer clear of lotteries or any kind of gambling, and stock markets, because you have little chance of winning in such opportunistic games.

In summary, a good nose is high, straight, unbiased, with a round nose tip, hidden nostrils, and large wings. Generally, a high nose is superior to a flat nose, a round tip is superior to a pointed tip, invisible nostrils are superior to visible ones, and a straight bridge is superior to a crooked bridge. However, care must be exercised in reading the nose. It must be read against a wider context of the face. That is to say, it must be in proportion to the size and length of the whole face, i.e. the principle of harmony and balance. Thus, while a high, big nose is an auspicious sign, it can mean disaster and frustration if it is set in a small face with receding cheekbones. This will have a negative effect on one's fortune because it violates the principle of harmony and balance.

Like its classification of eyes, the art of Chinese face reading draws heavily upon the principle of man-animal resemblance in the understanding of various kinds of noses, in addition to keen observation of the characteristics of individual noses.

On the following pages is a detailed list of such classifications.

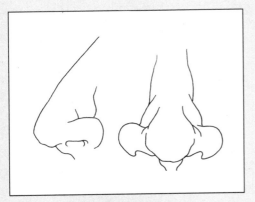

Figure 12.1: Dragon nose

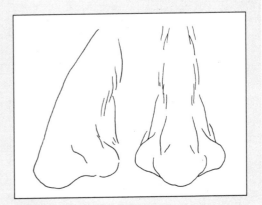

Figure 12.2: Rhinoceros nose

Dragon Nose

A dragon nose is one that has a long, high, and straight bridge, as well as a full, fleshy nose tip, with large wings but small nostrils. (See Figure 12.1.) It is the most prominent feature in the entire face. A dragon nose indicates great authority, power, wealth, and a beautiful or handsome spouse. Typically, emperors, presidents, and heads of state all have such a nose, or a very similar one. Founding Emperor Gaozhu of the Han Dynasty possessed such a nose. Emperors Meiji and Akihito of Japan all have such a nose along with Palestinian leader Yasir Arafat and former U. S. president Lyndon Johnson.

Rhinoceros Nose

A rhinoceros nose seems to extend straight into the forehead without a break. The bridge is extremely straight and high, and the nose tip fleshy and round. (See Figure 12.2.) Chinese face reading regards this kind of nose as a very auspicious sign. It symbolizes supreme power and authority in certain fields. The person is bound to be a leader, most likely in politics or the military. Many heads of state and great soldiers in history and modern times possess such a nose, for instance, former U. S. presidents Ronald Reagan and John F. Kennedy. Extraordinary success in career and finance, coming no later than in middle age, is guaranteed for those born with such a nose.

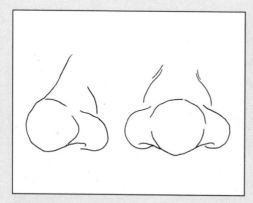

Figure 12.3: Lion nose

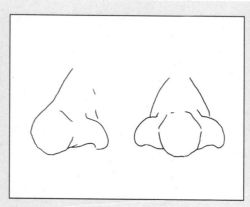

Figure 12.4: Bee nose

Lion Nose

A lion nose is characterized by a relatively flat bridge coupled with a very full, fleshy nose tip and wing, with invisible or partially hidden nostrils. (See Figure 12.3.) Such a nose signifies extraordinary power, wealth, fame, and tenacity. However, success will not come easily to those with a lion nose, although it is assured. Lion-nosed people have to fight harder for success than those with a dragon or rhinoceros nose. Typically, they will have a hard time before the age of forty-five. Until then, their careers will fluctuate, full of ups and downs. However, these are persistent people with strong self-confidence. Typically, they are self-made, and are able to foresee the bright linings behind the dark cloud, and they work tirelessly towards their goals. Not surprisingly,

they can all find success after a turbulent middle age. Business and politics are fields that are especially suitable to these people.

Bee Nose

A bee nose is very similar to a lion nose. The difference lies in that the bee nose is not as fat in nose tip. (See Figure 12.4.) Like a lion nose, a bee nose also symbolizes authority, wealth, and honor. In fact, both are considered leadership types of nose in Chinese physiognomy.

Tiger Nose

A tiger nose is similar to a rhinoceros nose in that both have high, straight bridges that extend almost directly into the forehead. The difference lies in that a tiger nose has a

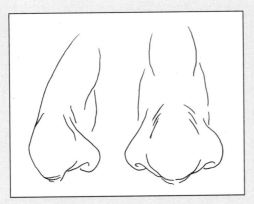

Figure 12.5: Tiger nose

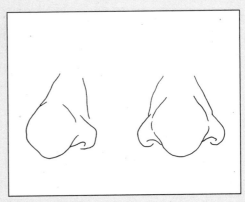

Figure 12.6: Garlic nose

broader bridge and smaller wings. (See Figure 12.5.) A tiger nose is an indication of foresightedness, courage, decisiveness, and high social position. People with such a nose are very energetic, ambitious, and courageous. They are capable of great deeds in times of war or peace. Those with tiger noses are also blessed with honor and authority. They can be very lucky with money, although money is not a priority in their lives.

Garlic Nose

A garlic nose is a very full and fleshy nose tip falling at the end of a small, short nose bridge—similar to the image of a bundle of garlic cloves. (See Figure 12.6.) While similar to a lion nose, a garlic nose has much smaller wings. It is a symbol of great material wealth, gained through hard work after middle age. Those with a garlic nose are very money-oriented with strong business acumen. Generally, a lion nose is preferable to a garlic nose.

Big Bladder Nose

A big bladder nose has a long bridge and a very plump nose tip with relatively small wings. (See Figure 12.7, page 124.) It is so named because it looks similar to a gall bladder. As ugly as it may look, owners of such a nose are considered lucky because it signifies great wealth and a beautiful spouse. It may be why men with ugly noses often end up marrying beautiful ladies.

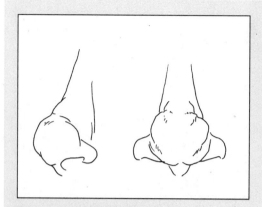

Figure 12.7: Big bladder nose

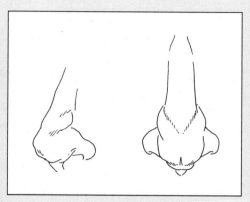

Figure 12.8: Small bladder nose

Small Bladder Nose

This kind of nose possesses all the qualities of its larger counterpart above, only in a smaller magnitude. (See Figure 12.8.) As in the case of a big bladder nose, a small bladder nose indicates the guaranteed wealth, although on a lesser scale, and marrying a beautiful spouse. If a small bladder nose is accompanied by a pair of good ears, its owner can compete with that of a big bladder nose in wealth and fame.

Ram Nose

A ram nose has a plump nose tip with fleshy wings. The nose bridge is fairly long but somewhat bumpy. (See Figure 12.9, page 125.) Such a nose indicates wealth and a big family.

Cow Nose

A cow nose has a short bridge, round nose tip and fleshy wings with partially hidden nostrils. (See Figure 12.10, page 125.) Such a nose indicates wealth and artistic taste as well as diligence and a logical, orderly manner in the pursuit of objectives. Oftentimes, people with cow noses are self-made. Wealth comes slowly but surely to them, along with a happy family and a capable spouse.

Eagle Nose

This nose is so named because it resembles the beak of an eagle: a high, arched bridge and a nose tip that is sharply hooked and pointed, falling below the level of the nostrils. (See Figure 12.11, page 125.) Owners

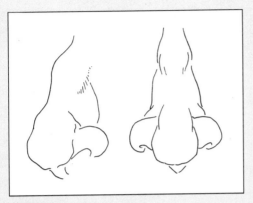

Figure 12.9: Ram nose

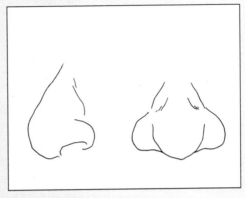

Figure 12.10: Cow nose

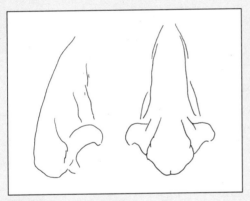

Figure 12.11: Eagle nose

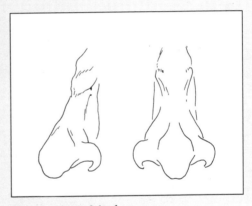

Figure 12.12: Monkey nose

of such a nose are by nature cunning, shrewd, sinister, and decisive. They can usually ascend to very high social positions, especially in politics and business. To them, the ends justify the means. They would not hesitate to step on others in promoting their own causes. While they are also very sexy and romantic, they have as little loyalty towards their spouse as towards their friends.

Monkey Nose

A monkey nose has one or more bumps in the nose bridge. (See Figure 12.12.) This

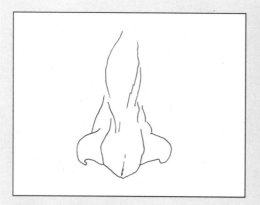

Figure 12.13: Zigzag nose

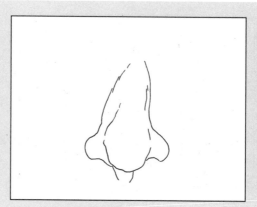

Figure 12.14: Biased nose

kind of nose signifies financial and relational turbulence, especially during middle age. It also indicates serious health problems in the middle age and a lonely character. Owners of such a nose have a great chance of getting divorced, going bankrupt, or suffering from severe illness in middle age. They are advised to keep a close watch on their purse as well as their health.

Zigzag Nose

This nose is obviously crooked and has two or more "twists" or "sways" in the bridge, with visible bones. (See Figure 12.13.) Such a nose indicates dishonesty in intentions, thinking, and motives. It also signifies frustration in wealth, relationships, and career. However, if a zigzag nose has a fleshy, round tip, the misfortune can be re-

duced, but the owner is a miser who cares more about money than anything else. If the tip is pointed, the owner must be a cruel opportunist who would not think twice about treading on others for his or her own advantage.

Biased Nose

This nose leans toward one side. (See Figure 12.14.) It indicates a biased way of thinking. Owners of such a nose often harbor evil intentions and like to "sow wild oats" in their youth. They may face a marriage crisis in their middle age. Also, they may have other legal problems during that time. Luckily, if the nose tip is full and round, the degree of evil intention and marital crisis can be significantly lowered.

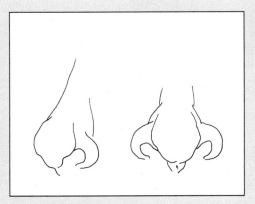

Figure 12.15: Pig nose

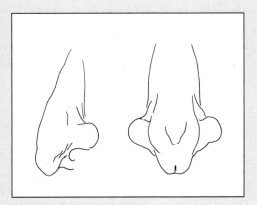

Figure 12.16: Goat nose

Pig Nose

The outstanding characteristic of a pig nose is the upturned nose tip, which makes the nostrils fully visible. (See Figure 12.15.) A pig nose indicates naiveté, honesty, and financial as well as emotional instability. Those with such a nose will encounter bankruptcy in middle age, and are likely to have an eventful, frustrating life. Financially, they can go from affluent to broke, with little being saved. Indeed, they have a hard time saving. Whenever they make big money, a lot of claims arise to compete for it, and pig-nosed people generally do not know how to prioritize.

Emotionally, owners will most likely encounter divorce or separation with their spouse. They are honest and friendly, but they will not become leaders.

Goat Nose

A goat nose is characterized by the superfluous flesh that hangs on the nose tip below the nostrils. (See Figure 12.16.) It signifies a lewd personality—a sexually greedy and selfish nature. Owners of such a nose usually are very lucky with the opposite sex, but this is bound to cause trouble in family life. Throughout their lives, they tend to have many boyfriends or girlfriends, but in the end, they still feel unsatisfied. Indeed, sexual drive is the strongest drive in their lives. All other things, power and money included, are subordinate to sexual desire, and are only used as a means to this very end. They are often caught in a "love triangle" situation, and can lose most of their fortune in sexual adventures.

	Nose Bridge	Nose Tip	Wings	Nostrils
Auspicious	high, straight	big, round	full, fleshy	invisible
Inauspicious	low, crooked, or bumpy	pointed	thin	visible

Table 12.1: Summary of criteria for noses

Chapter 13

Cheekbones

The cheekbones are known as the "power bones" in China. This is a very telling name, because these bones measure the scope and level of power one has, both at home and in society. Cheekbones also indicate personal authority and physical courage.

There are three types of cheekbones to look for: high cheekbones, cheekbones connected to the ears, and low, receded cheekbones.

High Cheekbones

Good cheekbones are set high on the face, fleshy, and round, like two guards protecting the face, especially the nose. (See Figure 13.1, page 131.) Such cheekbones indicate extraordinary courage, perseverance, strong willpower, and political authority. They are noted for their strong fighting spirit bordering on aggression and adventure, and a thirst for power and control over others. Therefore, most people holding high political or military positions are found to possess such cheekbones. In fact, most great soldiers of the world are born with high, prominent cheekbones.

An example of such a leader is General Zen Guofan of the late Chin dynasty who used to divide his fighting troops into three layers: the vanguard, the main body, and the rear guard, and fill these three layers with appropriate soldiers. Since the vanguard layer bears the brunt of enemy attacks, and their performance has great impact on the morale of the troops, and therefore, the outcome of the battle, it should be filled with soldiers with extraordinary physical courage. So Guofan made it a point to select only high-cheekboned people to form his vanguard troop, and left those with small cheekbones in the main body. Based on these tactics, he successfully suppressed the Taiping Rebellion, which far outnumbered him in the beginning.

Such cheekbones are not without their drawbacks. For one thing, owners of high cheekbones are sometimes too power-oriented, aggressive, and short-tempered. This may damage their popularity, although they do not seem to worry about that much, for many of them prefer to be feared rather than loved. It can be a hard task to deal with people with high cheekbones.

To be successful in politics and the military, however, high cheekbones themselves are not enough. They have to be accompanied by a high nose and auspicious eyes. If the cheekbones are high and projected, but the nose is small and pointed and eyes small and withdrawn, one cannot hope to go very far in the field of politics, and one's career will witness many ups and downs.

An example of this is the famous captain Li Guan of the Han dynasty who was a man of extraordinary courage, uprightness, and military talent. Li was credited with the driving out of Huns. For all his courage and feats, he hardly got any reward and promotion from the emperor. He died a disillusioned and disappointed man. Fathers of face reading tell us that Li was born with a pair of high cheekbones but had a small nose and eyes.

Traditionally, for a woman, high cheekbones represent a somewhat different story. They are considered an inauspicious sign for the happiness of the woman's family.

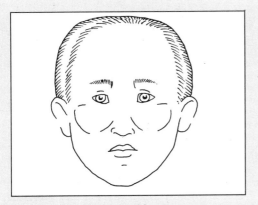

Figure 13.1: High cheekbones

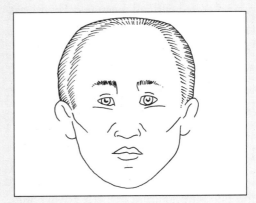

Figure 13.2: Cheekbones connected to ears

Again, this should be understood in the special context of timing and society in which the art of face reading was developed. According to traditional Chinese culture, such a woman is said to be bossy, controlling, and bad-tempered; such a personality could not but hinder the family. The woman will also not have a happy marriage. She will marry more than once, either because of divorce or because her husband dies early.

Many strong women in modern times possess such cheekbones. In fact, high cheekbones found in a female face these days are considered an auspicious sign, indicating that the woman can be very successful in her career and can have a very happy family life, as long as her husband does not possess too strong of a personality. Otherwise, they might find themselves in a situation in which "diamond cuts diamond." Such a family situation can cost both parties a lot of precious energy, which can be used more profitably elsewhere.

Cheekbones Connected to Ears

If the cheekbones are not just high, but extend to the ears, this is an unfailing sign of a military leader, with a visible tendency to kill and avenge. (Figure 13.2.) Such people are born for power, and would rather physically destroy challengers to their power than win them over. To many of them, the very meaning of life lies in power and control—to be sought with all means and protected with all measures. Their least favorable word is "retirement." If forced to retire, they will not live long afterward. Again, the rule applies that to be successful in politics and the military, high cheekbones also need a high nose and good eyes.

Low, Receded Cheekbones

Low, receded cheekbones exhibit exactly the opposite qualities of high cheekbones Cheekbones that are low and receded, or marred with moles or lines, inform a face reader of a conservative, withdrawn, and timid personality that would rather compromise than compete; they would sacrifice power or even money in exchange for peace and stability. (See Figure 13.3.) Competition is not in the blood of such people. They are more easily satisfied with the status quo and try to avoid violence. Their life philosophy is to go with the tide, and they admire the soft power of water which can, if patient and persistent, wear away a rock. Therefore, it would be a big mistake to undervalue their capacity for endurance and passive resistance, which can wear down a strong enemy with mild tactics.

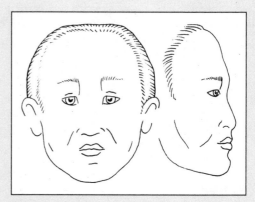

Figure 13.3: Low, receded cheekbones

If the chin is also pointed and receded, low-cheekboned people have even less fighting will and a weak sense of responsibility. Typically, they are despondent and pessimistic. They would try their best to avoid holding positions of high responsibility, preferring to be led by others. However, there is an old Chinese saying to the effect that trees want to be quiet but wind just blows nevertheless. For all their good will and sincere desire for a peaceful life, they may not get such a life in the end.

	Cheekbones
Auspicious	high, straight, round, and fleshy or high and extending to the ears
Inauspicious	low and receded, or marred by moles or lines

Table 13.1: Summary of criteria for cheekbones

Summary Reading #4: Nose and Cheekbones

Test your knowledge on chapters 12 and 13. Look at the photo of the popular world figure on the following page and try to read his face, specifically analyzing his nose and cheekbones. Then see how closely your analysis matches the author's interpretation.

Bill Clinton, forty-second president of the United States, first elected in 1992 and re-elected in 1996, led one of the most embattled administrations in the nation's history.

AP Photo/Greg Gibson

Bill Clinton

Nose: _____

_____

_____

_____

Cheekbones: _____

_____

_____

_____

Author's interpretation: To be sure, the most outstanding feature in this president's face is his nose. Clinton's nose is also the most auspicious facial feature, which deserves the greatest credit for earning him two successive terms as president. He has a typical garlic nose—pure and perfect, with a very fleshy, round nose tip and a pair of well-concealed nostrils, which are hardly visible. Moreover, Clinton's nose has a high, long, straight, and broad bridge—indeed, a superb nose.

Such an excellent nose signifies, among other things, a top government position, great authority, and international fame. Since the nose stands for one's middle age, it is little wonder that Bill Clinton should become the president of the United States in his forties—neither earlier nor later in his life—and is one of the youngest presidents in U. S. history.

The height, length, and straightness of his nose indicates that Clinton enjoys good health, possesses a very high level of energy, as well as an above-average personal wealth. This is because the nose is also the home of the Health Palace and the Wealth Palace.

What stands in his way to accumulate a lot of wealth in this lifetime are his ears, which are small and insignificant compared to his nose. The ears also speak of the material wealth one enjoys. Such being the case, he may make a lot of money in this lifetime, but in the end he will not have much to save. One way or the other, he will have to give up what he has earned in terms of money.

Clinton's cheekbones are round but not very protruding. Since the cheekbones stand for power, a Chinese face reader would reasonably expect to see them more outstanding in the face of a president. At first sight, this is somewhat confusing and perplexing to me as a face reader with an Asian background. I now realize that here is a typical example of the differences between an Eastern face and a Western face, and this difference can be as political as physical. There is simply no comparison between the personal power of a Chinese emperor and that of a U. S. president. Can you imagine a Chinese emperor forced to testify under oath in court? This is simply out of the question, because in China, the emperor himself is the law. With this in mind, you will not be surprised to find President Clinton having a pair of cheekbones which could be more outstanding. Especially when you compare his cheekbones with those of his wife, which are more protruding and powerful, you can be sure that the first lady is the "speaker of the Clinton house."

Before leaving, let us take a careful look at his eyes. Kind, mild, tender, shiny, smiling, and beautifully curved, Clinton's eyes indicate that this is a very kind-hearted person who cares immensely about social justice, particularly the welfare of the common American people. History will most likely remember him as the "President of the Common People."

永美命

Chapter 14

福 Philtrum

Vertically located between the nose and the upper lip, the philtrum is referred to in Chinese physiognomy as well as Chinese acupuncture as Renzhong, or literally, "the center of man." Despite its insignificance from the viewpoint of anatomy and modern medicine, the philtrum possesses a unique place in face divination, and within it lies rich information about one's health, social position, longevity, and family size.

Criteria used by fathers of Chinese face reading in their analysis of this facial feature include length, depth, coverage, and symmetry.

Figure 14.1: Long, deep, and covered philtrum

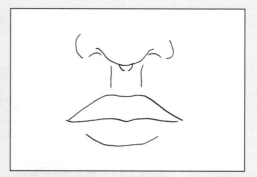

Figure 14.2: Short, flat, and uncovered philtrum

Long, Deep, and Covered

Fathers of face reading hold that good philtrums for males are long, deep, and covered with a beard. (See Figure 14.1.) The owner is said to be blessed with profound knowledge, a high social position, power, health, longevity, and a large family (Chinese ancients considered a large family indispensable to happiness and good fortune). One's livelihood will also be secured throughout one's life. Such a philtrum is a protection for its owner against evils. However, if the philtrum is just long and deep but devoid of a beard, the person may hold a very powerful position but will be deprived of offspring.

Since women typically do not grow mustaches, this type of philtrum will not apply to them. Interestingly though, Chinese fathers of face reading did note that any hair grown on a woman's philtrum indicated trouble in marriage and possible divorce, as well as sour relations with family members and solitude in old age.

Short, Flat, and Uncovered

A short, flat philtrum without a beard on a male face will contribute to a low social position, frustration in career, short life, and few children. (See Figure 14.2.) Even if children are born into the family, they will either die young or become juvenile delinquents, bringing disgrace to the family. If the philtrum is not only flat, but dark and dim as well, the person is in danger of death soon, either to illness or an accident.

Once these qualities are determined, we then look at the symmetrical aspects of the philtrum and other, specific characteristics.

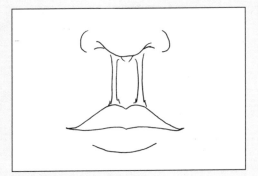

Figure 14.3: Parallel philtrum

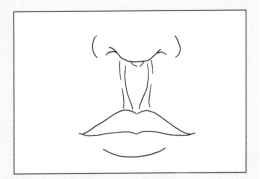

Figure 14.4: Wide top philtrum

Parallel

Another type of philtrum is parallel on both sides, i.e., it is the same width from top to bottom. (See Figure 14.3.) Such a philtrum indicates administrative talent and diplomatic skill. If the philtrum is not only parallel on both sides, but long in itself, one is sure to hold a high social position and have promising children, who are going to be successful and bring honor to their parents.

Wide Top

Another type of philtrum is one that is wider in the upper portion but narrows toward the bottom. (See Figure 14.4.) This is referred to as a philtrum with a head like a tiger but a tail like a snake. Such a philtrum indicates a fine start but a poor finish

in life. In other words, owners of such a philtrum are usually happier in the first half of their lives than in the second half. They may encounter bankruptcy or some other sudden deterioration in wealth or health in the later part of life. Another meaning of this kind of philtrum is that the person will have children early in life.

Wide Bottom

By far the more common type of philtrum is where it is wider at the bottom than the top. (See Figure 14.5, page 142.) Just as people grow in knowledge as they advance in age, this type of philtrum indicates maturity and presence of mind. Wealth, like knowledge and experience, comes slowly but more steadily to the owners of such a philtrum. They also tend to marry late in life and so do their children. Relationships between parents may undergo some crisis in their childhood. This is because the top of the philtrum corresponds to early stage of life, and a narrow upper part means a tougher time for the person during child-hood.

Occasionally, some people have a philtrum that slants toward one side. This indicates that these people will bring bad luck to their family members, most likely to their children.

If moles are found in the philtrum, the person may have reproductive problems. This is mostly true in females. Some face readers take it as an indication of death in the water, and warn those with such a

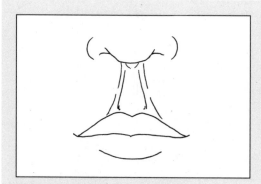

Figure 14.5: Wide bottom philtrum

philtrum to stay away from large bodies of water as much as possible. (See chapter 20 for more information on moles.)

	Length	Depth	Coverage	Symmetry
Auspicious	long	deep	beard	parallel
Inauspicious	short	flat	bare	biased

Table 14.1: Summary of criteria for philtrums

Chapter 15

福 Mouth

The mouth performs two important functions—eating and communication—that to a large extent determine our health, success, and relationships. An ancient Chinese saying tells us that "diseases enter the body through the mouth; disaster springs out of the mouth." Little wonder that so important a facial feature constitutes a lengthy topic of discussion in Chinese face reading.

The mouth can tell a lot about one's relationships with others. As mentioned in chapter 5, the mouth is also the location of the Relations Palace. As the commander of communication, the mouth can promote as well as destroy a relationship in a moment's notice. In fact, many good relationships have gone sour because of words, intentional or unintentional. This is exactly what is meant by the Chinese saying.

For women, traditionally, the mouth indicates children. A good mouth indicates good children while a bad mouth would, obviously, indicate bad children or children dying young. Good children are children who will be successful later in life, and who are respectful of and obedient to their parents. Bad children are those who become involved in drugs or crimes, are hostile and ungrateful to their parents, or simply show no affection at all.

Although many types of mouths have been classified by the fathers of face reading, some qualities of the mouth can be generalized to give us a broader understanding: color, thickness, shape, symmetry, and open versus closed.

Color: Color is an important quality when analyzing the mouth. It is an indicator of your health as well as your relationships with others. Rosy lips signify good health, an optimistic attitude toward life, and generally good relationships with others. White or dark lips, on the other hand, signify ill health, pessimism, and strained relationships. Generally speaking, people with rosy lips often have more friends than those with dark or white lips. This is partly because optimistic, outgoing people make

friends more easily than pessimistic ones. This criteria regarding the color of lips are universal, applicable to all ethnic groups.

Thickness: As a general rule, thin lips signify conservatism and determination. Those with thin lips are not very good at expressing their feelings and emotions. They tend to be harsh, revengeful, and even cruel at times. They are decisive and oftentimes considered cold-blooded by others because they are hardly given to sentiment or emotion. Reasoning and logic with the goal of profit and productivity are their governing drive. They usually have good communication skills, a sharp mind, and are quick to respond or retaliate in verbal terms. They do not have many friends, especially long-term ones.

If just the upper lip is thin, it is a sign of financial straits. If the lower lip is thin, it indicates trickery and unreliability in terms of promises or friendships.

If the lips are thick, the person is more honest, simple, loyal, and friendly. Such a person may be awkward in speech, but will be rich in feelings and affection, making more reliable friends. The drawbacks of those with thick lips include the tendency to give themselves to emotion and excessive sexual indulgences. Thick lips indicate an energetic life full of emotions and feelings. People with thick lips are often very emotional, and are therefore more subject to emotional ups and downs, and more easily hurt by relational setbacks. When they fall in love with others, they want to be fully engaged, heart and soul, and demand the same from their partners. These people are also more demanding sexually. In other words, they have a stronger sexual appetite than others. Affection is to them what water is to fish. For them, it is inconceivable that life can exist without love and affection.

Shape: A third criteria for the mouth lies in its shape. Again, strict distinction is laid down in this regard between yin and yang, or the male and the female. The ideal mouth shape for a man should be broad and square while closed, but round while open. Fathers of Chinese face reading believe that in order to be respected and hold a high government position, which in traditional Chinese society used to be regarded as the first thing to be desired in terms of good luck, a man should have this type of mouth. There is a famous saying to the effect that a square mouth ensures livelihood throughout the world.

It is said that the founding emperor of the Tang dynasty had a mouth so wide and majestic that it could accommodate his own fist with ease. The late president Chiang Jinguo of Taiwan had exactly such a mouth. Fathers of face reading hold that

such a mouth is conducive to supreme power and authority, in addition to material affluence throughout life.

If the mouth is small as well as dark, and turns downward at both corners, the owner cannot go far in his career and will encounter poverty and poor health later in his life. However, if the mouth is only small but not dark, it can be a good thing because it can mean a person who is considerate of others. Such a personality often leads to good interpersonal relations and deep love between the spouses. This is especially the case when the mouth is not only small, but rosy as well.

Symmetry: Face divination also observes that if the upper lip is longer than the lower one, one's father will die before one's mother, whereas if the lower lip is longer than the upper lip, the mother will die first. If the two lips do not fit to each other, i.e., they do not match or close well against each other, or they are slanted or skewed, it is a sign of shrewdness, lies, and broken promises. This criteria applies to both genders.

Open or closed: A good mouth must be able to fully cover the teeth when closed which is considered normal and has no special meaning. If the mouth remains open to a certain degree and the teeth are visible as a consequence, it indicates that the person is a troublemaker, whose talkative nature often turns into the habit of saying bad words about others. It also signifies that the person has a sour relationship with almost everybody, including dear ones. Those with such a mouth will often find themselves being the target of verbal attacks. This is especially the case as they gain some success and fame, or when a scapegoat is needed for some wrongdoing committed by others. This quality applies to both men and women.

So in general, for a male, a good mouth is thick, broad, square, sanguine, slightly turning upwards at both corners, and fully covers the teeth. For a female, an auspicious mouth is one that is small, thick, round, rosy, upward turning, and well-balanced.

Following is a list of different types of mouths identified in Chinese physiognomy.

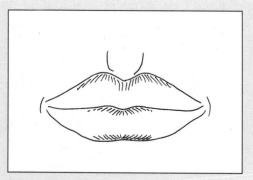

Figure 15.1: Dragon mouth

Dragon Mouth

A dragon mouth is one that is big and wide with prominent corners, and the lips are full and even. (See Figure 15.1.) Such a mouth indicates wealth, honor, power, and access to delicious foods to enjoy throughout life.

Bow-shaped Mouth

A bow-shaped mouth is one that turns upward at the corners, giving the image of a bow. (See Figure 15.2, page 149.) To be a genuine bow, the lips should also be red and thick and the teeth white. Such a mouth signifies wealth and honor and friendship. Those with bow-shaped mouths are blessed with intelligence, communication skills, lasting friendships, and wealth. They will have good foods to eat throughout their lives. Their old age is ensured to be happy

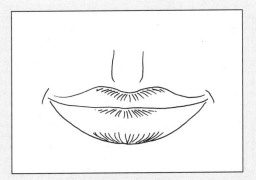

Figure 15.2: Bow-shaped mouth

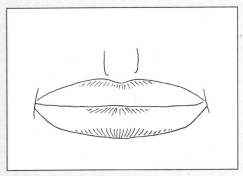

Figure 15.3: Character "Four" mouth

and rewarding, even if other parts of the face are not so favorable. This is considered as one of the best types of mouth for women to have.

Character "Four" Mouth

This mouth looks similar to the Chinese character "four" when closed, i.e., it is very wide, with a clear rectangular shape, thick and red lips, and upwardly turned corners. (See Figure 15.3.) Such a mouth indicates great wealth, high social position, as well as an extroverted personality. People with such a mouth are very sociable and loyal, making friends easily. They are also optimistic, self-confident, resolute, and courageous. These traits help explain why they are successful in their careers and finances. They easily earn the trust of their superiors

and respect from their subordinates—indeed, this mouth is a symbol of strong leadership. Plus, they will have delicious foods to enjoy throughout their lives.

Tiger Mouth

A tiger mouth is broad, thick, rosy, symmetrical, and conspicuously wider in the center than at the ends. (See Figure 15.4, page 150.) Such a mouth is often found on people who have considerable inheritance, strong perseverance, and high intelligence. It also indicates generosity and abundance of emotions. It is also a symbol of wealth and good luck in enjoying delicious foods throughout life.

If the teeth are also well covered, such a mouth signifies great honor and high social position. People with such a mouth make

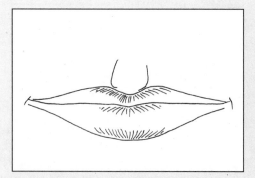

Figure 15.4: Tiger mouth

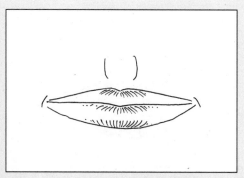

Figure 15.5: Character "One" mouth

good partners, both in business and in sex. As business partners, they are generous with their colleagues relative to money. As sex partners, they will devote a lot of their time and energy to making the other person happy in bed. If they become leaders, they will be considerate of the welfare of their subordinates.

Character "One" Mouth

This mouth resembles the Chinese character "one," which looks almost like a straight line. (See Figure 15.5.) The lips are thin and straight, symbolizing great determination, strong communication skills, and the willpower to excel and control. People with this mouth are often power-oriented. They enjoy being in leadership positions and they make quick, strategic decisions. On the

down side, they may be too task-oriented to the detriment of the welfare of others. Indeed, they can be very selfish and unsympathetic.

Monkey Mouth

A monkey mouth is wide, thin, and curved. (See Figure 15.6, page 151.) Such a mouth indicates a person with extreme cunning and an opportunistic personality. Masters of face reading find that such a mouth often belongs to opportunists who are as diplomatic as they are scrupulous. They are decisive and have little hesitation in adopting extreme measures in promoting their causes; they have a strong appetite for money and power. They also have a hard time making and keeping friends.

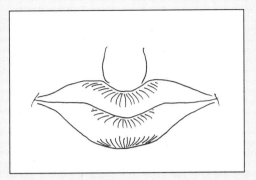

Figure 15.6: Monkey mouth

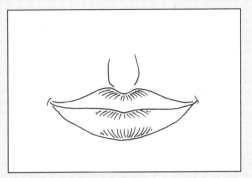

Figure 15.7: Cow mouth

Cow Mouth

A cow mouth is thick and red but relatively small, with the corners turning upward. (See Figure 15.7.) It tends to be very large when the person laughs. The entire shape looks very beautiful and well-balanced. Such a mouth indicates health, wealth, a happy marriage, and an affectionate and artistic character. Owners of such a mouth are said to be blessed with good health, delicious foods, and many other material comforts. They love money, but regard it as a means rather than an end in itself. While optimistic most of the time, they can be very sentimental occasionally. When they make friends, they will try to keep the relationships throughout their lives. These people are very popular with the opposite sex, and tend to lead a romantic lives.

Fish Mouth

A fish mouth is small, thick, and protruding, with indented corners. (See Figure 15.8, page 152.) Such a mouth indicates an introverted personality. People with this type of mouth tend to be reticent and pensive. When they do speak out, they are brief and to the point. To them, adjectives and adverbs are redundant. As such, they often cause misunderstandings, especially with their romantic partners. Also, these people have a tendency to alcoholism, because they find alcohol an aid in helping them communicate their introverted mind.

Bird Mouth

A bird mouth is similar to a fish mouth in that both are small and protruding, except a bird mouth is thinner. (See Figure 15.9,

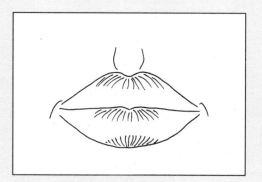

Figure 15.8: Fish mouth

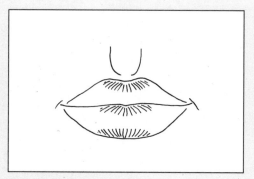

Figure 15.9: Bird mouth

page 152.) This mouth indicates a very talkative character; people tend to say more than is proper. This will cause them a lot of trouble, possibly turning out to be fatal to their careers or even their lives.

Wrinkled Mouth

Just like it sounds, this mouth has many wrinkles or lines on the lips, which have little to do with aging. (See Figure 15.10, page 153.) Owners of such a mouth tend to lead lonely but long lives. They are pensive, profound thinkers with sharp insight and intuition, but their communication skills may not be very good.

Cherry Mouth

A cherry mouth is small, rosy, with a thick lower lip that turns upward at the corners.

(See Figure 15.11, page 153.) This mouth indicates an emotional, gentle personality gifted with extraordinary intelligence and artistic talents, which, if properly explored, can lead to fame and wealth. Such a mouth is highly recommended for a female. Fathers of face reading hold that women born with such a mouth can be good wives and enjoy honor, wealth, and prosperity.

Pig Mouth

A pig mouth is small and protruded with thick lips. (See Figure 15.12, page 153.) Such a mouth indicates a lazy character and indulgence with material comforts. These people are said to be lacking in patience and courage and have short tempers. Many find themselves in trouble because of their careless speech. Money comes and goes with them, and they may have trouble making

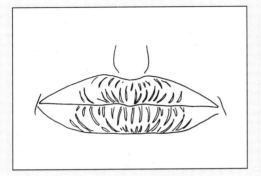

Figure 15.10: Wrinkled mouth

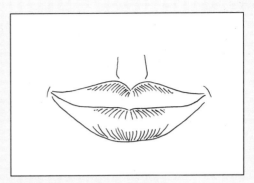

Figure 15.11: Cherry mouth

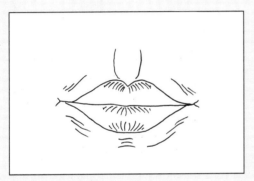

Figure 15.12: Pig mouth

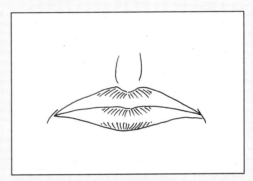

Figure 15.13: Mouse mouth

both ends meet late in life. In times of need, these people can expect little help from others, including family members. They have to find a way out for themselves.

Mouse Mouth

This mouth is small with thin lips and corners slanting downward. (See Figure 15.13.) Such a mouth indicates meanness, narrow-mindedness, poverty, misery and an opportunistic attitude. Those with mouse mouths enjoy commenting on the private affairs of others, and are jealous of those with success and good luck. On the plus side, they are usually very alert and sensitive to opportunities and threats in the environment, and have a good mastery of details, but a poor understanding of the overall picture.

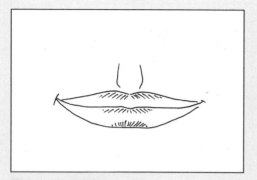

Figure 15.14: Ram mouth

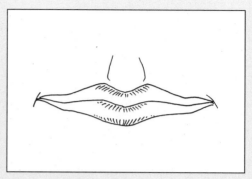

Figure 15.15: Fox mouth

	Color	**Thickness**	**Shape**	**Symmetry**	**Open/Closed**
Auspicious	rosy	thick	broad, square	balanced	closed
Inauspicious	white, dark	thin	small	unbalanced	open

Table 15.1: Summary of criteria for mouths

Ram Mouth

A ram mouth is small and thin with the corners turning upward. (See Figure 15.14.) Such a mouth indicates a cautious and conservative but optimistic nature. Those with ram mouths are very good at tactical and logistic planning, and they can be good accountants and business people.

Fox Mouth

This mouth is large and wavy with at least two twists. (See Figure 15.15.) It indicates a dishonest, cunning, and lecherous character. Although eloquent, those with fox mouths have a hard time convincing people of what they say, because their ideas change so often. They tend to eat their own words. They take great pleasure in their sexual prowess and are usually very successful. They are also inclined to marry several times.

Summary Reading #5: Philtrum and Mouth

Test your knowledge on chapters 14 and 15. Look at the photo of the popular world figure on the following page and try to read his face, specifically analyzing his philtrum and mouth. Then see how closely your analysis matches the author's interpretation.

Martin Luther King, Jr. was a Baptist minister who became a prominent civil rights leader during the 50s and 60s, until he was assassinated in 1968.

AP Photo

Martin Luther King, Jr.

Philtrum: _____

_____

_____

_____

_____

Mouth: _____

_____

_____

_____

_____

Author's interpretation: Well-educated, confident, and courageous, Martin Luther King, Jr. once commanded the attention and admiration of people all over the world. A mere look at his face will convince a Chinese face reader that this was no ordinary person.

Equally impressive and extraordinary were his philtrum and mouth. The philtrum indicates one's health status, children, social position, and personality. Although his philtrum was largely covered by a mustache in the picture, we can still see that it was straight, long, and deep. Such a philtrum signified an upright personality, good physical health, high energy, good children, and a prominent social position. His excellent physical health matched his superb mental power. Such a philtrum also ensured that his family tree would continue on unbroken for generations, although his own life would be cut short by his assassination.

As if this was not enough, his mouth follows up with a promise that he will live in the hearts of people long after his death. In Chinese physiognomy, the mouth is indicative of one's personality, social status, eloquence, reputation, and luck with food. King's was a character "four" mouth—wide, rectangular, and thick, with majestic corners that turned slightly upward. Such a mouth revealed an eloquent and extroverted personality, great wealth, high social position, national or international reputation, and both the love of, and luck with, good food.

While I did not see King in person, I have heard recordings of his speeches where his voice was loud and sonorous. King was probably the most eloquent voice of the civil rights movement. No one could so effectively and vehemently light the fire in the hearts of his audience—white or black—against social injustice and racial discrimination as he did.

We are told that he was short of stature. If so, this is more evidence pointing to his predestined great success. Here was a man short in stature but gigantic in thinking and voice. It is no coincidence that King should establish his lasting career and reputation largely by means of his mind and mouth.

Looking at his other facial features, almost all are extraordinary. His forehead—broad, high, and protruding—clearly indicated that King was endowed with excellent intelligence, if not genius, as well as intuition and drive that would affect the lives of millions. He came from a good family background, and earned his Ph.D. at an admirable age of twenty-six. More significantly, from the perspective of physiognomy, it was a matter of course that he should achieve great success and fame in his thirties. This was largely due to his superb Life Palace and Career Palace.

Looking at his Life Palace, this space between his eyebrows was extremely wide. Moreover, it was smooth, free from any marks, and slightly protruding. It indicated a strong life force, great ambition, and a high probability of achieving great success in one's thirties.

This high probability turned into certainty by King's excellent Career Palace which, like his Life Palace, was broad, round, shiny, and protruding. As the name implies, the Career Palace indicates one's success in career, but also one's imaginative and intuitive power. King's Career Palace was perfect. The combination of a superb Life Palace and a perfect Career Palace ensured that he must be very successful in his thirties. Fate did work its way for this man in a timely, punctual manner. He was honored with the Nobel Peace Prize at the age of thirty-five, one of the youngest people ever to win this laureate.

永 美 命

Chapter 16

福 Teeth

You may be surprised to find that teeth are also analyzed in Chinese face reading. Teeth are considered the "pillars of the mouth," meaning they are supporters of, and intimately associated with, the mouth. The teeth reveal information about relationships, whether or not one will have a stable livelihood, access to delicious foods, and the quality of family life. The characteristics and meanings can be applied to both men and women.

Chinese face reading holds that teeth should, preferably, be long, straight, closely set, white, orderly, and lie flat, neither protruding nor receding. Such teeth indicate a long life, good relations, security of livelihood, intelligence, and honor.

Color: Teeth that are as white as ivory symbolize a high government or business position, career success, a good reputation, and happy relationships. On the other hand, teeth that are dark (yellow, stained, or marked), short, loosely set, or small in size indicate poor relationships, dishonesty, a short life, uncertain financial situation, and changing fortunes.

Number: The number of teeth one has is also important. The general principle is this: the more teeth one has, the luckier one will be. Emperors and empresses are believed to possess thirty-six teeth, premiers thirty-four teeth, ministers thirty-two teeth, and those with above-average good luck and secure livelihoods, at least thirty teeth. Any number below thirty is considered a sign of mediocrity and poverty.

Symmetry: Other characteristics to look for in the teeth are uneven shapes and gaps. If the teeth are wider on top but pointed at the bottom, it is a sign of avarice and cruelty. Owners of such teeth are likely to be carnivorous with an unpredictable character. On the other hand, if teeth are wider at the bottom than on the top, the person is likely to be a vegetarian and kind-hearted.

Gaps between the teeth indicate wealth coming and going, as well as the inability to keep a secret. One should think twice before confiding in such a person something extremely important and sensitive.

Special attention is also paid to the two front teeth. There is even a special name for them—the Inner School teeth. The Inner School teeth affect not only one's fate, but one's personality as well. To be considered good and auspicious, the two front teeth should be straight, large, long, white, and closely set. Such teeth indicate longevity, good social position, fame, and trustworthiness.

If the Inner School teeth are short, crooked, pointed, yellow or black, or have a visible gap, the owner tends to be mean and very dishonest, often given to cheating even their best friends. Such a person is not to be trusted, especially in matters of life and death. Such people often think of taking advantage of others to promote their own interests. Unfortunately, they often outwit themselves, because such front teeth also signify a short, turbulent life full of ups and downs in their wealth and poor relationships with others.

If the Inner School teeth are auspicious but the rest of the teeth are not, it's literally a tie—nothing typically lucky or unlucky happens.

A face reader should also be aware of any major dentistry done to the teeth, such as caps, crowns, or bleaching. If there are such changes, the face reader should ask what the teeth were like before the major dentistry and go from there.

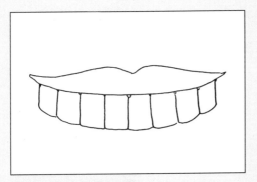

Figure 16.1: Jade teeth

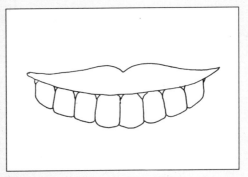

Figure 16.2: Pomegranate teeth

The following is a list of various kinds of teeth and their respective significances.

Jade Teeth

Jade teeth are white, large, and closely set against each other. (See Figure 16.1.) They are considered to be very auspicious because they indicate fame, wealth, happy relationships, health, and longevity.

Pomegranate Teeth

These teeth are round at the bottom and closely set. (See Figure 16.2.) The upper row forms a bell-type curve because the middle teeth are longer than others. Such teeth indicate that the person is intelligent, has a lot of delicious food to eat, and little trouble finding a spouse in one's lifetime.

Leaking Teeth

Leaking teeth are loosely set against each other with obvious gaps in-between. (See Figure 16.3, page 162.) They are indications of financial and relational instability. The gaps symbolize the leakage of money and information. Of course, if the nose and mouth are good, this negative effect will be minimized.

Devil's Teeth

These teeth are so called because they are so crooked and "zigzagged" in appearance that almost no order can be detected. (See Figure 16.4, page 162.) Such teeth indicate a mean-spirited nature, jealous and calculating, as well as health and relational problems. Those with devil's teeth are often frustrated in money and love affairs, and can expect little help in times of difficulty.

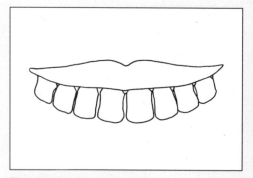

Figure 16.3: Leaking teeth

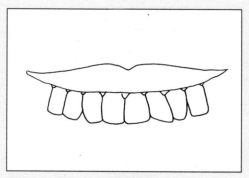

Figure 16.4: Devil's teeth

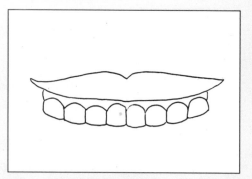

Figure 16.5: Swollen teeth

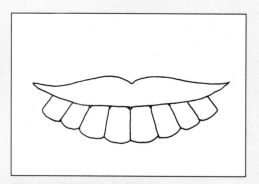

Figure 16.6: Outwardly turned teeth

Swollen Teeth

The name here may cause some misunderstanding, because it is not the teeth that are swollen, but the gums surrounding the teeth. So much so that the teeth are overly covered by the gums and look shorter than they should. (See Figure 16.5.) Such teeth indicate that the person does not have a high intelligence and can be mean in dealing with others.

Outwardly Turned Teeth

If the teeth turn outward, away from the center, it is an indication of an outgoing personality and success away from the homeland. (See Figure 16.6.) Usually, owners of such teeth are self-made people who set up their careers and families far away from home.

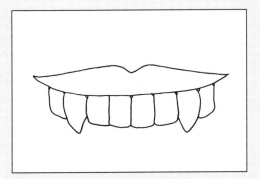

Figure 16.7: Dog teeth

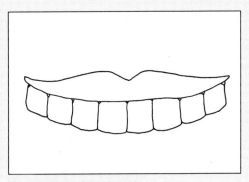

Figure 16.8: Broad teeth

	Color	Size	Number	Symmetry
Auspicious	white	long, large	more than thirty	straight, closely set
Inauspicious	yellow, dark	short, small	under thirty	uneven, gaps, widely set

Table 16.1: Summary of criteria for teeth

Dog Teeth

Dog teeth are characterized by unusually long, pointed teeth on both sides of the upper four middle teeth. (See Figure 16.7.) Dog teeth indicate a person who will bring bad luck to their dear ones, especially parents and spouses.

Broad Teeth

If the teeth are broad and wide, they indicate honesty, excellent energy, good appetite, an open mind, and an outgoing personality. (See Figure 16.8.) People with such teeth make better friends than those with narrow teeth. Unfortuantely, they may often find themselves taken advantage of by others, so they should be careful in their selection of friends.

Chapter 17

福 Chin

In Chinese face reading, the chin is referred to as the "earth portion" of the face. It lies at the very bottom of the face, and is therefore related to the period of old age. This portion of the face carries an unusually heavy significance in Chinese physiognomy. Together with the philtrum and the mouth, the chin constitutes the entire lower portion that determines one's welfare and fortune after fifty. This is the time when people seriously think about retirement and social security; this is also the time when people have most of their health problems. Therefore, a good chin signifies an auspicious old age with the security of money, relationships, children, and good health.

From the viewpoint of face reading, a good chin is fleshy, broad, protruding, and turning upwards. In Chinese physiognomy, a chin that turns upwards is known as "the heaven and the earth facing each other." (Here heaven stands for the forehead.) If this is the case, it is a very auspicious sign, indicating that the person will enjoy a happy old age, in which the strong tide of fortune will bring wealth, fame, and all kinds of comforts to the person. Indeed, a good chin is considered God's best guarantee against a miserable old age.

A full, fleshy, and broad chin suggests a strong willpower and sexual drive, as well as a fondness for worldly comforts. Those with such a chin will "sow a lot of wild oats" in their lifetimes. Their material lives in old age will also be comfortable; that may be part of the reason why they enjoy their old age so much.

A chin is inauspicious if it is thin, short, pointed, and receding. Such a chin indicates, in most cases, an old age characterized by financial strains, loneliness, and/or poor health.

It is said that Zhu Yuanzhang (1327–1398), the founding emperor of the Ming dynasty, possessed a chin that looked like a big spoon that turned up toward his forehead. The physiological significance of this extraordinary chin is historically confirmed, for Zhu died a happy emperor with hundreds of millions of subjects and hundreds of thousands of square miles of land under his control. Coming from a family of poor peasants, Zhu was the only survivor of a family of eight and entered a local Buddhist temple to earn a living. The managerial monk of the temple happened to be an experienced face reader and recognized in Zhu a great future despite his contemporary poverty and ignominy.

The chin is more important to a woman than a man, just like the forehead is more important to a man than to a woman. This is because in the Chinese philosophical system, the forehead corresponds to heaven which in turn symbolizes man, while the chin corresponds to earth which in turn symbolizes woman.

A good female chin is round, thick, large, preferably doubled, and protruding. Such a chin indicates happiness, wealth, and longevity. Women with such a chin are found to be devoted to love and family. A pointed chin indicates that she is stern in appearance but kind at heart. A rectangular chin, as in the square or broad types listed below, signifies a stubborn character.

Following are several different types of chins and their meanings that generally apply to both men and women.

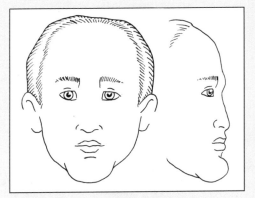

Figure 17.1: Protruding chin

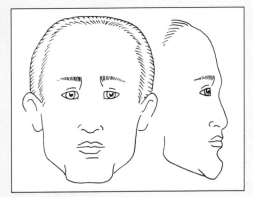

Figure 17.2: Square chin

Protruding Chin

A chin that protrudes toward the forehead is a clear indication of strong willpower and orientation toward power. (See Figure 17.1.) This is especially the case when the chin is not only protruding, but long and broad as well. People with such chins are leaders in their fields. Their careers are usually at their best after the age of fifty-five. It is the retirement age that brings them the most satisfaction in terms of power and glory. They are bound to have a happy, rewarding old age no matter what they do. Also, they tend to have big families with many children and grandchildren.

Square Chin

If the chin is square and broad, it indicates strong determination and sexual power, wealth, and a happy old age. (See Figure 17.2.)

Double Chin

The common misunderstanding is that a double chin is a natural result of being overweight. Actually, this is not true, for double chins can be found on those who are not fat at all. (See Figure 17.3, page 168.) A double chin indicates comfort, professional success, and financial security in old age, in addition to a strong desire for food and sex. The lucky thing for these people is that they can realize what that want and desire.

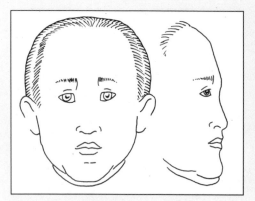

Figure 17.3: Double chin

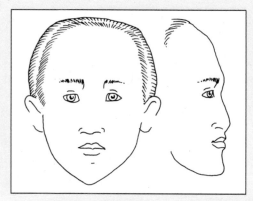

Figure 17.4: Pointed chin

Pointed Chin

If the chin is short and pointed, the owner is unlikely to live over seventy, with his later days being miserable. (See Figure 17.4.) Either the person will suffer from a painful disease, be involved in an accident, or go bankrupt. In the worst case scenario, the owner may die a violent death. For sure, old age is bound to be unhappy and eventful. For a woman, a pointed chin traditionally means she will likely have a very lonely old age, either because her husband dies, or they divorce, or she is deserted by her children.

Receded Chin

If the chin recedes rather than protrudes, it indicates an old age full of pessimism, a passive attitude towards life, a lack of spirit and sexual vitality, financial straits, and relational frustration. (See Figure 17.5, page 169.)

Long Chin

A long chin indicates business acumen, skills at practical affairs, and a long life. (See Figure 17.6, page 169.)

Round Chin

A round chin signifies material affluence, a good appetite for both food and sex, love of travel, and financial security in old age. (See Figure 17.7, page 169.)

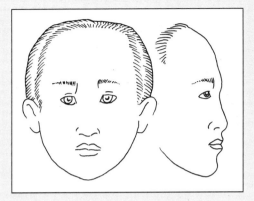

Figure 17.5: Receded chin

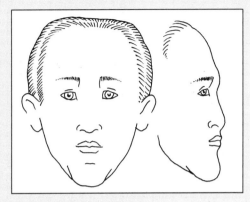

Figure 17.6: Long chin

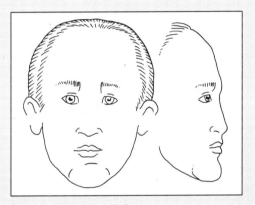

Figure 17.7: Round chin

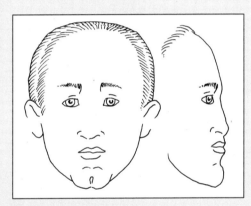

Figure 17.8: Broken chin

Broken Chin

If a chin is broken, meaning it has a visible perpendicular line down the middle of it, it is an indication of a lewd personality, and trouble in romantic and family relationships. (See Figure 17.8.) People with broken chins often marry more than once. Even if the chin is full and long, complicated relationships will spoil an otherwise happy old age.

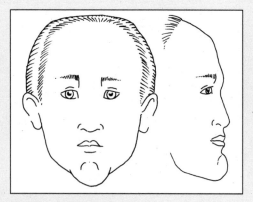

Figure 17.9: Mounted chin

	Chin
Auspicious	full, fleshy, broad, long
Inauspicious	thin, short, pointed, receding

Table 17.1: Summary of criteria for chins

Mounted Chin

This chin has a distinctive mount (a protruding bone), which stands out against the nose. (See Figure 17.9.) A mounted chin usually belongs to one who is capable of both making good money and spending it luxuriously. It also indicates a person with a strong sexual drive but has complicated sexual relationships, which often result in more than one marriage.

Summary Reading #6: Teeth and Chin

Test your knowledge on chapters 16 and 17. Look at the photo of the popular world figure on the following page and try to read her face, specifically analyzing her teeth and chin. Then see how closely it matches the author's interpretation.

Margaret Thatcher was England's longest-serving prime minister in the twentieth century. She was elected in 1979 for the first of three terms. She was Prime Minister until her resignation in 1990.

AP Photo/John McConnico

Margaret Thatcher

Teeth: _____

_____

_____

_____

Chin: _____

_____

_____

_____

Author's interpretation: This "Iron Lady of the West" boasts a mouth of "iron teeth": clean, white, long, closely set, and large in number. Unable to physically count the number of teeth in her mouth, I can very much tell by the size of her mouth and how close her teeth are set against each other, that she has no less than thirty-four teeth. In Chinese physiognomy, this is the number of teeth required for a premier, which she had been for three successive terms. To a large extent, her extraordinary teeth help reveal the secrets about her extraordinary life and career: clean, strong, long, and outstanding.

Such a set of excellent teeth speaks of several things for Mrs. Thatcher. For one thing, she is endowed with a very high intelligence. This is shown by her two front teeth (Inner School teeth), which are conspicuously bigger than her other teeth. For another, she is gifted with robust health and an abundance of energy, and will enjoy a long, healthy life. This is because long, white, and strong teeth signify good health, strong energy, and longevity in Chinese physiognomy. This was absolutely necessary for this extraordinary lady, for the job of a prime minister was one of the busiest in the world. It required excellent health and a high energy level in order to work long and irregular hours, travel frequently, and tackle a host of state as well as personal affairs in an orderly way.

It is said that Mrs. Thatcher only needs an average of four hours of sleep each day, half the amount needed by most people—another token of genius, if you will. No doubt, her excellent health status and energy level have contributed a lot to her success and outstanding performance during her long career as prime minister.

Her teeth also tell us that she enjoys a very happy family life. In Chinese face reading, teeth indicate, among other things, one's relationships with other people, most significantly with one's spouse and family members. In fact, this lucky lady can boast of a warm family and an understanding and devoted husband, in particular.

This same set of strong, broad, and long teeth indicate unusual courage, moral and physical. Mrs. Thatcher's perserverence to stand up for what she believes in, even in the presence of formidable obstacles, is her distinctive trademark. It is this trait that more than likely earned her the title "Iron Lady of the West."

Her chin, which is long, fleshy, and protruding, possesses most of the qualities for an auspicious chin, which indicates several things. First, she possesses substantial real estate and properties. Second, she has a large number of followers and subordinates—the chin is where the Servant Palace is located. Last but not least, she will enjoy a comfortable, affluent old age, since the chin represents the last stages in life. Her lasting reputation will also be excellent.

永美命

Chapter 18

Hair and Beard

What do hair and beards have to do with luck? It may sound ridiculous, but the quality of the hair and the beard do affect fate. They are still considered parts of the face and head, and therefore contain some important information about our lives.

While hair and beards are different things, the criteria used in their judgment are roughly the same. There are five criteria to look at: color, style, condition, thickness, and hairline.

Hair

The following criteria and characteristics generally apply to both men and women.

Color: Understandably, as a unique product of the Chinese culture, face reading regards black as the normal color of hair. Occasionally, a Chinese person is born with red hair. This is interpreted by fathers of face reading as an indication of early death.

While white hairs are a natural result of the aging process, hair that is prematurely white before the age of forty is a clear sign of health problems and legal troubles in their twenties. However, if the hair turns black again, it is a very lucky sign.

If the hair is blonde, it indicates that one will bring bad luck to close family members. If the hair is red, the person will be haunted by a lot of disasters in life.

If the person colors or dyes his or her hair, no conclusion whatsoever can or should be made based on that color. Even if they tell you what their original hair color is, it is totally meaningless for face reading, for both color and time have changed. We just cannot see to their original color through their colored hair as it stands now, nor can we be sure that even if they had not colored their hair, their original color of hair would remain unchanged. The only thing we can do is to draw no conclusion at all from this perspective. No conclusion is better than a misled, inaccurate conclusion.

Of course, modern face reading should take into account the ethnic background of the person being read to determine what color is normal for that ethnicity.

Style: Straight hair, considered the norm, is preferable to curly hair. If the hair is permed or styled curly, then it makes no difference, and it is not considered an inauspicious sign.

Curly hair is a sign of a strong desire for and indulgence in sexual pleasures. It is also an indication of a shrewd nature. Those with curly hair are more calculating and diplomatic in character. Unfortunately, such hair indicates some kind of misfortune in life, such as legal trouble and the separation from a spouse in the latter part of life. To be sure, their diplomatic personalities can help promote their interpersonal skills, but such skills are considered to be one of the most cynical characteristics by the ancient Chinese. Sages only ask us to be sincere, not skillful and diplomatic, in our dealings with others. In fact, some may be very skillful in their dealings with others, but there is little sincerity involved in the process. They merely use the skills as a means to promote their own interests. On the other hand, some are very shy and unskillful in dealing with others, but their motives are pure and sincere.

Since straight hair is considered the norm or standard for Asians, it carries little physiognomic meaning, indicating nothing particularly good or bad.

Again, ethnic background must be borne in mind when reading on an international scale. For any ethnic group, the style of hair that is stereotypical of that group is considered normal and therefore neutral in physiognomic meaning. In other words, such a hairstyle bodes nothing auspicious or inauspicious for people belonging to that ethnic group.

Condition: Good hair should be lustrous, soft, and naturally fragrant. Lustrous, shiny hair is preferable to dry, dull hair in that it is a sign of strong qi and blood energy inside the body, and therefore contributes to the good luck of the person. For women with such hair that is also long, it is also a sign that they will enjoy good health and longevity, and be capable of delivering healthy babies.

Dry, dull hair indicates a deficiency in qi and blood energy, weak health, and a lot of worries throughout life. For women with such hair that is also short, it can indicate that she will marry more than once, and her marriages will not be happy. She will also have to double her efforts in order to make both ends meet.

Soft hair is preferable to stiff hair in that the soft is an indication of good luck and leisure in life. Owners will have an easier, more comfortable life because they do not have to work hard in order to make financial ends meet. Typically, they have an easier time than stiff-haired people in getting a good job, securing help from others, and earning a living for themselves. In this sense, soft hair means soft money and an easy life.

On the other hand, hard, stiff hair means hard work, a lonely nature, hot temper, and loss of money or even a spouse. Those with stiff hair have strong personalities and easily get involved in verbal arguments and physical fights with others at the slightest provocation. However, they are more frank and straightforward in their feelings than others and incapable of "playing under the board."

Thickness: The fourth criteria is the thickness of the hair. By thickness is meant how much hair there is on the head. Chinese fathers of face reading tell us that hair should neither be too thick nor too scarce. This is quite contrary to medical understanding of the thickness of hair, which holds that a thick head of hair is an indicator of good health whereas thin hair or a bald head is indicative of health problems. In face reading, thick hair indicates bad luck, a lot of worry in life, and unthankful labor.

Thin hair, where the scalp is slightly visible, is considered a very auspicious sign in that the owner will easily find happiness in life. They only need to work half as hard as their thick-haired counterparts in order to have the same degree of success. This is more true if the hair is thinning later in life. Hence the physiognomic saying in China that there is no thick-haired premier, nor is there a bald-headed premier.

While too much hair is an inauspicious sign, premature baldness is not good either, for premature baldness may be caused by some health problem. However, if baldness comes after the age of fifty, it can also signify extraordinary intelligence. In fact, many great Chinese scholars and philosophers are bald-headed, among them being Confucius, Lao Tze, and Zhuang Tze.

Even the way one balds makes a difference. If one starts balding from the forehead and progresses backward, it is considered a good sign. If the balding starts from the middle or back of the head, it is an inauspicious sign of health problems, and often indicates that the person will not live a long life.

Hairline: This has a lot to do with the quality of the forehead. While judging hair from this perspective, one should bear in mind the physiognomic difference between male and female. For a male, it is desirable that the hairline be well receded, leaving a broad, high forehead visible. Hair should not cover the temples or come close to the eyebrows.

For a female, however, too much forehead is normally considered an inauspicious sign in terms of happiness in relationships and marriage. Therefore, her hair should grow relatively closer to the eyebrows in order to have a harmonious family life.

Hair that grows in the ears indicates intelligence and longevity. Such a person is quick to learn and understand, but may lack persistence in anything they do. He or she may be given to the luxuries and comforts of life. Oftentimes, people with hair in their ears are found to waste away their precious energy in search of fun. So long as they do not go to extremes and know the limit, they will be able to enjoy a long life.

Beards

A beard is considered a variation of hair in China and a universal male symbol. It is believed that no one can be regarded as a perfect man without a beard. Just like a pair of eyebrows is the masculine sign of a young man, a "forest of beard" is the masculine sign for an elder man. Therefore, it is desirable to have a beard, especially one that covers the philtrum and chin. No beard at all indicates weak sexual vitality, a lack of children, and a lonely personality. This also includes mustaches. If a person has just a mustache but not a beard, it can mean declining fortune in the later part of life or even a violent ending.

	Color	Style	Condition	Thickness	Hairline
Auspicious	black	straight	lustrous, soft	thin, scalp slightly visible	receded
Inauspicious	blonde, red, prematurely white	curly	dull, dry, stiff	thick	not receded

Table 18.1: Summary of criteria for hair and beards

Like hair on the head, a good beard is black, lustrous, and soft, but long. Such a beard contributes to wealth and longevity. However, if the beard is dry and stiff, it indicates a headstrong character and bad luck with money. If it's a long, white beard decorating the chin, it helps make one's old age smooth. All of the other rules of color for hair are applied to beards as well.

Generally speaking, unlike hair, the thicker the beard, the more energetic and sexy one will be. Full-bearded people are considered very energetic, active, productive, and efficient. However, they have the tendency to waste a lot of their energy on worldly pleasures; their mind is always busy with professional or romantic projects.

While the lack of a beard itself is indicative of weak sexual vitality, it can also indicate an indulgence in sex if it is coupled with a pair of very meager, pale eyebrows. In fact, many famous womanizers are found to have little beard and eyebrows for they indicate a libidinous nature.

If the beard and eyebrows join forces at the temples, it is an inauspicious sign indicating that the person had a very hard childhood, has a poor family background and is potentially in danger of fatal accidents, either by car or in water.

永美命

Chapter 19

福 Moles

M oles are also important indicators of fate. Former chairman Mao Tse-tung, for instance, had a big mole on the left side of his chin. That mole was a very auspicious sign for his political career. Liu Bang, the founding emperor of the Han dynasty, had seventy-two black moles on his left leg, thus, associating moles with the mandate of Heaven. However, not all moles are good signs; in fact, some can be very bad, even fatal. Hence the importance of careful differentiation.

First of all, Chinese physiognomy holds that invisible—not readily visible—moles are auspicious and preferable to visible moles. Invisible moles include those that are hidden in the eyebrows, hair, beard and mustache, and on the body. To see such moles, a Chinese divinator would have to spend more time and look more closely at the clients, often with his hands to temporarily move away the hair or clothing in order to discern what is hidden under them.

Secondly, when reading moles, it is very important to keep in mind the principle of yin and yang. A mole in the same facial location on a man and a woman can mean different things. Because of this, there are two different mole systems based on gender. Figures 19.1 (page 183) and 19.2 (page 185) illustrate these two systems. It is the location, not the quality, of the moles that matters. Therefore, these mole systems illustrate exact locations of moles in order to obtain a correct interpretation of them.

A detailed explanation of what these moles mean is listed as follows, beginning with the male face.

Males

Refer to Figure 19.1 on page 183 as the moles are discussed, beginning with the forehead and moving down the face, from left to right.

1. The five moles on the forehead (from left to right) signify misfortune in travel, death in the battlefield, high government position, good compensation, and impediment to parents, respectively.

Moles in the hair are indications of wealth and longevity. This can be moles hidden in the hair, in the beard, in the mustache and in the eyebrows.

Moles in the eyebrows signify great wealth.

A mole in the Life Palace, i.e., between the two eyebrows, signifies good luck and high social position.

Moles found on the eyelids are indicative of a hard life full of troubles and disappointments.

2. The six moles located above the left eye (moving from left to right) indicate loss of money, misfortune, disaster in water, good luck, misfortune, and honor, respectively.

3. The five moles above the right eye signify (from left to right) great honor, good social position, disaster in water, misfortune, and loss of money.

4. The five moles below the left eye mean (from left to right) suicide, early death of sons, no offspring, few sons, and treachery.

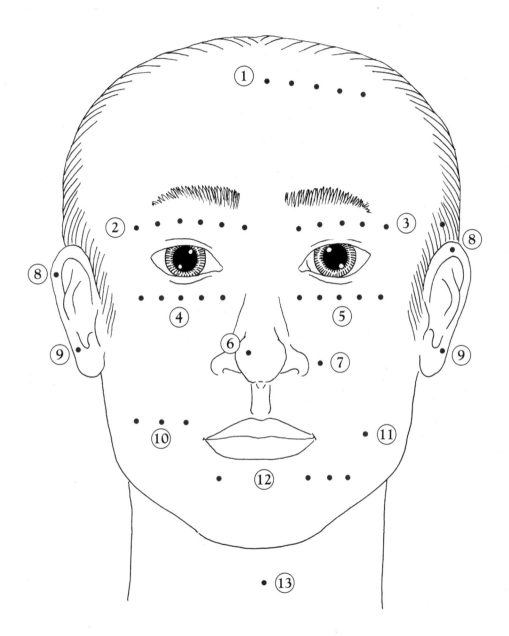

Figure 19.1: Moles on the male face

5. The five moles below the right eye mean (from left to right) licentiousness, few daughters, many miserable occasions, early death of father, early death of spouse.

   Moles grown on the nose bridge or right beside the nose signify diseases and frustration in career or political ambitions.

6. A mole on the nose tip indicates loss of money, bad luck for one's family members, and a violent death.

7. A mole on the right wing of the nose indicates disaster in water. A mole on the left wing signifies loss of money.

8. Moles on the upper part of the ears indicate good luck and wealth.

9. Moles on the lower part of the ears indicate high intelligence and longevity.

   Moles in the philtrum signify easiness in finding a spouse.

   Any mole in the lips indicates that the person loves food and is lucky in the enjoyment of good food throughout life, with a tendency to become an alcoholic.

   Moles on the lower lip signify loss of money and frequent arguments with others.

10. The three moles to the left of the mouth indicate death far away from home.

11. A mole to the right of the mouth indicates upstart in career or wealth after middle age.

    A mole found in the mentolabial sulcus, the dented location right below the mouth, signifies death by alcoholism or alcohol-related accidents.

12. The four moles on the chin indicate (from left to right) intelligence, alcoholism, good luck, and a happy old age, respectively.

13. Moles on the neck signify high social position, especially in the military.

Females

Refer to Figure 19.2 on page 185 as the moles are discussed, beginning with the forehead and moving downward, from left to right.

14. The ten moles on the forehead indicate (from the left to right) wife of a tycoon, multiple marriages, impediment to parents, poor family background, second marriage, harm to relatives, impediment to husband, death away from home, harm to husband, and disaster at delivering children.

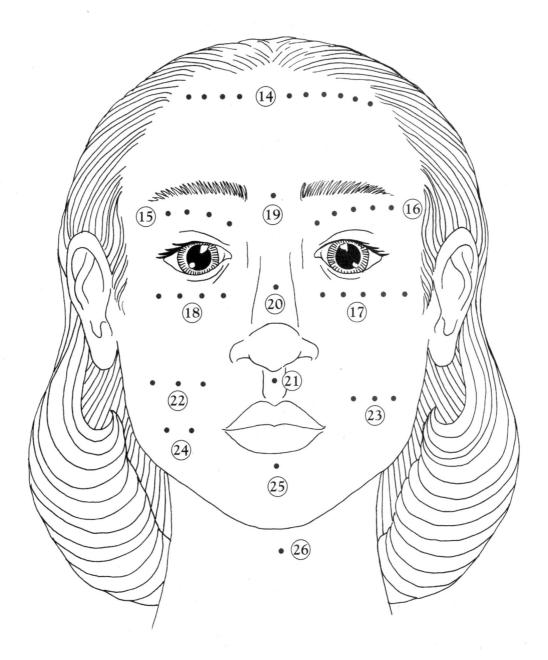

Figure 19.2: Moles on the female face

15. The four moles below the left eyebrow indicate (from left to right) good luck, divorce, an asset to husband, and prison terms.

16. The five moles below the right eyebrow signify (from left to right) good luck in textile business, helpfulness to children, good husband, harm to husband, and a long life.

17. The four moles under the left eye signify (from left to right) strong sexual desire, husband survived by wife, impediment to children, and accidents.

18. The five moles under the right eye signify (from left to right) a thief, good luck, treachery, few children, and disaster in fire.

19. Moles grown between the eyebrows indicate harm to the husband.

20. A mole on the nose bridge signifies disaster and disease.

    A mole on the nose tip indicates that the woman will have to work hard after marriage, either because her husband is lazy, or because he is poor and deep in debt, or because he is mentally or physically sick.

21. If a mole is located at the upper part of the philtrum, it indicates fertility.

    If a mole appears in the middle of the philtrum, it indicates divorce. If it is found in the lower part of the philtrum, it speaks of adultery and a loose character. If there are two moles in the philtrum, it is a sign of giving birth to twin babies.

22. The three moles to the left of the upper lip signify suicide, jealousy, and water disaster, respectively.

23. The three moles to the right of the upper lip mean bad luck to children, strong desire to win, and bad luck to husband.

24. The two moles to the left of the lower lip indicate disaster in water and hardship in life.

25. The mole just below the mouth, at the indent, indicates lack of property.

26. Moles grown on the neck indicate misfortune for the husband.

永美命

Summary Reading #7: Hair, Beard, and Moles

Test your knowledge on chapters 18 and 19. Look at the photo of the popular world figure on the following page and try to read his face, specifically analyzing his hair, beard, and moles. Then see how closely your analysis matches the author's interpretation.

Fidel Castro, a Communist revolutionary, has been Cuba's president since 1976.

AP Photo/Jerome Delay

Fidel Castro

Hair and beard: _____

_____

_____

_____

_____

Moles: _____

_____

_____

_____

Author's interpretation: The outstanding feature of Cuban leader Fidel Castro's face lies in his thick, full, and curly beard, which seems to grow everywhere, especially since it connects with his thick hair. Such a beard reveals a combination of interesting personalities.

For one thing, it indicates a rebellious nature deeply rooted in disrespect for the status quo and other's authority. Such a person often turns out to be a leader in times of political turmoil. In fact, Castro not only disrespected the social order before he came to power, but actually led an uprising against the government in 1953, the failure of which earned him a prison term while he was still in his twenties.

Also indicated by his full, curly beard is a restless mind and a hot, impatient temper, which can easily turn into burning jealousy if not controlled. In his best light, he has a powerful personality with an iron willpower and an unshakable determination to achieve his objectives in leading his country. At his worst, he nurtures a strong inclination toward absolute power.

Chinese physiognomy also sees in this full beard a person endowed with an abundance of energy, both mental and physical. This is an important reason why Castro has achieved so much in his life, especially in his political career. But this abundance of energy can be a double-edged sword. On the positive side, it empowers its owners to work efficiently for long periods of time. On the negative side, it may lead its owners to find an easy outlet for their pent-up energies through indulgences. Castro seems to have stricken a perfect balance between the two extremes. While a hard-working and effective leader, he is said to greatly enjoy the company of beautiful women. Actually, he himself once told reporters that he has many girlfriends, and proudly praised Cuban women as being "very, very sweet." This may be just a means to an end, which is to balance his nervous and tense mental world.

Besides his affluent beard, we also notice quite a few moles on his face. Some of the moles are located on the Spouse Palaces, others are hidden in his eyebrows, and still others are on his forehead. Those located on the Spouse Palaces are a clear indication that this is a man who can bring misfortune to his wife, if he chooses to marry. Such misfortune can take various forms, including but not limited to, miscarriage, mistreatment, or divorce. The moles hidden in his eyebrows signify material wealth, and the pair of moles lying in symmetry on the forehead above his eyebrows tells us that this is a man who has achieved great power and authority in the early half of his life.

Chapter 20

福 Lines

Fathers of face reading also call attention to the lines on the face, which we call wrinkles. By means of intuition or imagination, the masters have successfully established the link between these lines and their location on the face to information regarding fate in life.

It is believed that lines can be favorable or unfavorable. The meanings of the lines depend on their location on the face and their shape. The following pages discuss various lines and their meanings, beginning with the forehead and moving downward, from left to right. Refer to Figure 20.1 on page 193, which illustrates some of the more commonly found lines on a face.

A single horizontal line across the forehead is called the Canopy Line, which indicates literary talents, hard work, and loneliness of character

1. Two horizontal lines crossing the forehead are called Lying Moon Lines. They indicate middle-level government positions and above-average power.

   Three horizontal lines on the forehead that are roughly parallel to one another are called Unicorn Lines. These indicate honor of very high government positions and great power.

   Vertical lines in the center of the forehead indicate solitude.

2. Vertical lines on the left side of the forehead indicate that one's siblings will die in places far away from home.

3. Vertical lines on the right side of the forehead signify impediment to one's siblings.

4. A "cross" formed by two perpendicular lines that appears anywhere on the forehead signifies wealth and prosperity, while a series of crosses on the forehead is a sign of a high government position.

5. A zigzag or crooked line crossing the forehead is called the Snake Crawling Line, which signifies a serious accident or even death during travel.

   Three zigzag lines crossing the forehead indicate that one's father will die before one's mother when that person is still young.

   Lines that cross each other on the forehead indicate poverty and misfortune.

6. A vertical line running from the Life Palace (between the eyebrows) all the way up through the forehead to the hairline is called the Heavenly Pillar Line. It indicates a high government position.

   Two vertical yet parallel lines running from the Life Palace up to the forehead are called Crane Feet Lines. They indicate the position of a governor.

   A short, vertical line in the Life Palace indicates strong willpower and diligence, as well as legal troubles and possibly divorce. If there are two vertical lines found in this location, it is an auspicious sign of honesty and good social position. Three vertical lines are a sign of longevity.

7. Lines in the left eyelid indicate that one's mother will die a painful death.

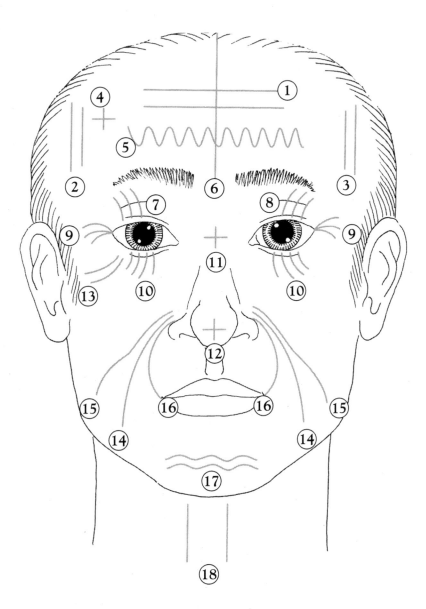

Figure 20.1: Common lines in the face

8. Lines in the right eyelid indicate that the father will meet a violent death. These lines are seen when the eye is open and they must be deep.

9. Lines at the outer corners of the eyes indicate complexity in romantic relationships, which can mean either divorce, extramarital affairs, or death of a spouse. If many lines are found at the outer corners of the eyes, the person has to work very hard in life. Also, such a person will have sex appeal even at an old age.

10. Lines immediately below the eyes mean misfortune for one's children.

11. Lines found at the uppermost part of the nose bridge, vertical or horizontal, are an indication that the person will experience difficulties in his or her late thirties and early forties.

   Lines appearing on the upper part of the nose bridge signify that the person's parents and grandparents might have a large fortune, but the fortune will be lost in the hands of that person.

   Vertical or horizontal lines appearing on the lower part of the nose bridge signify misfortune at around the age of forty.

12. Vertical or horizontal lines found on the nose tip indicate a cruel nature and frustration in pursuing many ambitions.

13. Lines on the cheekbones indicate a second marriage, which will most likely come in the mid-forties.

14. Of particular interest are the two symmetrical lines flanking the mouth on both sides. In the parlance of Chinese physiognomy, they are called falins, or literally the "orders of law." Falins, or lines of authority, represent power and authority, and real power and authority at that. This means that they not only have the position and title but also the real authority to have their orders followed by others. People playing the second or third fiddle in an organization are sometimes found to have the position and title, but only symbolic authority; they are respected more than obeyed.

   Falins alone cannot tell the whole story about one's power and authority. Falins must be read in conjunction with other facial features such as the cheekbones, eyes, and nose. Thus, if the eyes are weak, the nose bridge broken, or the cheekbones flat, good falins can only mean power and authority over one's children, hardly even over one's spouse. But, if the other features are good and the falins are weak, one is a task-oriented person, and does not have the stuff for real leadership.

Strong falins mean strong power over others. These favorable falins are straight, long, and deep, extending all the way along both sides of the mouth to the end of the chin. Such lines indicate real authority and the ability to have orders followed. It is no wonder falins are usually found in the faces of those in leadership positions, military leaders in particular. Fathers of Chinese face reading asked emperors to use lines of authority as an important criterion in the selection of generals.

Short, crooked, and shallow falins are considered unfavorable. People with these kind of falins are not suitable for leadership positions, least of all in the military. After all, to lead and order means to have real power and authority. In its absence, chaos and confusion would arise among the ranks.

The degree of authority is reflected in the length, depth, and straightness of the lines of authority. In other words, the longer, deeper, and straighter the lines, the more powerful the person in terms of having his orders carried out.

15. If the falins are not only deep and long, but also far apart from each other, i.e., there is quite some distance between the falins and the mouth, such people usually have a strong tendency to impose their will on others, including fellow peers. These people are very aggressive and assertive.

If a falin turns into two lines, i.e. forks, this symbolizes dual authority-power and authority in different fields such as civilian and military affairs.

16. Occasionally, we find people who have falins running directly into their mouths. In Chinese physiognomy, this is called "snake entering the mouth," and is a very inauspicious indication that these people will have to struggle to live past the age of fifty.

17. Lines on the chin indicate danger in the water, meaning you will have an accident in the water that may cause death.

18. Two horizontal lines running parallel to each other on the neck indicate military power. If there is only one line, there is no special meaning.

Chapter 21

Bones

In general, bones in the head tell us what level of power and authority one has. It is held that if there are no special bones in the head, one cannot hope to ascend very high in the government, including the military. Bear in mind that in traditional China, a high government position is considered superior to anything else in terms of luck. Part of the reason for this is because China was a feudal country in which man, not law, ruled. As long as you have political power, you have everything—wealth, women, honor, whatever. Since political power comes out of government positions, such positions are therefore held to be the first priority in fate. Of course, this refers almost solely to men, because women typically did not hold government positions in traditional China.

Studying the various bones in the head is a subtle subject because the bones are less obvious than the other facial features. To accurately measure and appropriately judge the bones often requires the use of your hands in addition to your eyes. Move your hands across the head. If you can feel something standing up or protruding, it is considered a bone even though it is hard to see. This is the principle of implicates at work, meaning something that can hardly be seen but is actually existing.

Also keep in mind the principle of balance and harmony: if the head is small but some of the bones are exceptionally big, or if the person is small in stature but the head is very big, these are unlucky signs indicating a vicious temper and poverty.

It is repeatedly observed and confirmed in Chinese society that most people holding high government positions have special bones in their heads—some of these bones being explicit, while others implicit, i.e., hidden in the hair. This leads many face readers to believe that "there is no bad bone in the head." Unfortunately, this is an overstatement.

Bones can be auspicious and inauspicious depending on their shape and their location on the head. In terms of shape,

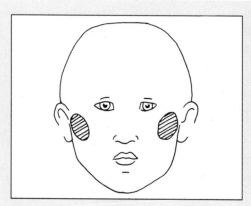

Figure 21.1: Cheekbones

head bones should appear rounded. Pointed bones are not desirable, even if found in the right location, for good luck is significantly reduced.

In terms of location, there are ten different kinds of auspicious bones classified, along with three types of inauspicious bones, which are listed on the following pages. Generally, these can be applied to both men and women.

Cheekbones

Cheekbones stand for power—political, military, or financial. Therefore, the bigger the cheekbones, the greater the power one has. (See Figure 21.1.) See chapter 13 for a more detailed discussion of cheekbones.

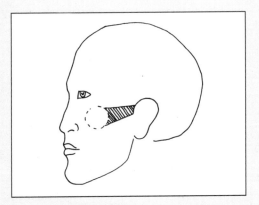

Figure 21.2: Horse bones

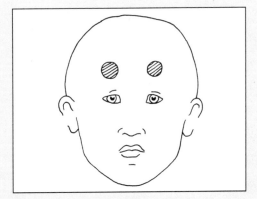

Figure 21.3: Sun and moon bones

Horse Bones

These are extensions of the cheekbones, extending all the way to the ears. (See Figure 21.2.) They indicate longevity, high governmental positions, and great power, military power in particular. People with visible horse bones will possess great power and live to at least eighty-five. Chiang Kai-shek and Deng Xiaoping, both had horse bones.

Sun and Moon Bones

This pair of symmetrical bones is located immediately above the eyebrows. (See Figure 21.3.) The bone on the left side is called the sun bone and the bone on the right side is the called moon bone. They indicate great power and authority.

Jade Bones

These are the two symmetrical bones surrounding the eyes. (See Figure 21.4, page 200.) They signify power and social position, which can mean anything from a mayor to a governor.

Heavenly Pillar Bone

This bone "stands up" in the middle of forehead, extending up into the hairline. (See Figure 21.5, page 200.) It indicates great power and authority, which can mean the power held by a minister at national level and above, or a three-star general and above if one is in the military.

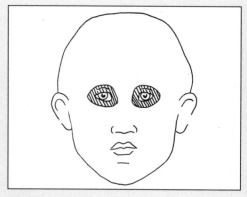

Figure 21.4: Jade bone

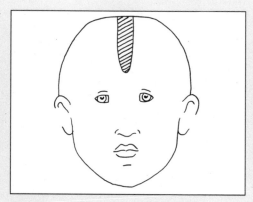

Figure 21.5: Heavenly pillar bone

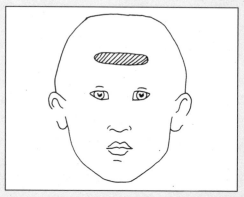

Figure 21.6: Tiger bone

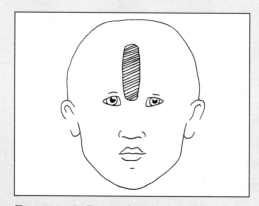

Figure 21.7: Dragon bone

Tiger Bone

The tiger bone is a bone that lies horizontally in the center of forehead. (See Figure 21.6.) It is an indication of special talents and of receiving special favor from the head of state.

Dragon Bone

This is a bone that vertically extends from the top of the nose bridge all the way up into the forehead. (See Figure 21.7.) It is an indication of supreme national power, either a head of state or a top official in the

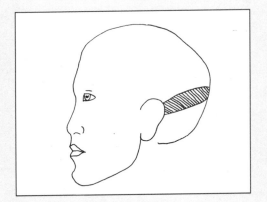

Figure 21.8: Shark bones

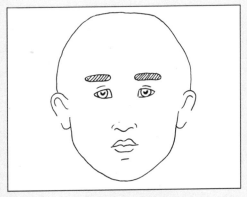

Figure 21.9: Supporting bones

administration. In ancient China, this meant either the emperor or the premier. My observation is that other high ranking officials can also have such a bone. While all those with a dragon bone will not always hold the position of premier, they do have a good chance of becoming a premier one day

Shark Bones

These two symmetrical bones are found behind the ears and extend all the way to the back of the head. (See Figure 21.8.) They symbolize great military power, and are therefore indicative of generals and marshals.

Supporting Bones

These two symmetrical bones are found right on the eyebrows. (See Figure 21.9.) They indicate a very high position in the government, often playing the role of directly supporting the head of state, hence the name. However, people with such bones are often fierce and have a short temper.

Back Bones

As the name implies, these are bones located in the back of the head. They can assume various shapes or forms: a horizontal line across the back of the head; a triangle or a crescent (see Figure 21.10, page

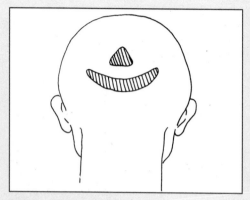

Figure 21.10: Back bones

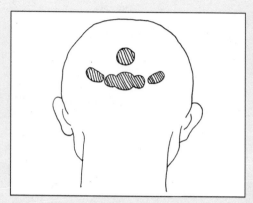

Figure 21.11: Back bones

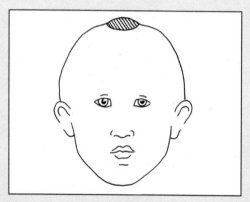

Figure 21.12: Lonely bone

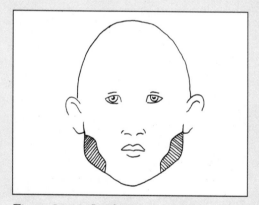

Figure 21.13: Jaw bones

202); a cross; and circles (see Figure 21.11). All kinds of back bones indicate intelligence and power, but the best ones are those with the shape of a circle or triangle.

A circle is best because it symbolizes perfection. A triangle is also good because it symbolizes stability.

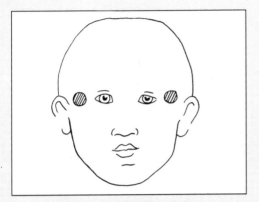

Figure 21.14: Spouse Palace bones

	Shape	Location
Auspicious	rounded	(see list on pages 200–203)
Inauspicious	pointed	jawbones, top of head, temples

Table 21.1: Summary of criteria for bones

However, not all bones found in the head are considered auspicious. The following are bones that are considered to be *inauspicious*.

Lonely Bone

This bone protrudes from the top of the head. (See Figure 21.12, page 202.) It indicates solitude and poverty in old age.

Jaw Bones

Big jawbones indicate a cruel, greedy, and selfish person who will not hesitate to step on the toes of others, including his friends and coworkers in order to benefit oneself. (See Figure 21.13, page 202.)

Spouse Palace Bones

These bones are located at the temples. (See Figure 21.14.) If these bones are found standing out in a face, it is an indication that the person is of a fast character and will bring bad luck to the spouse.

Summary Reading #8: Lines and Bones

Test your knowledge on chapters 20 and 21. Look at the photo of the popular world figure on the following page and try to read his face, specifically analyzing his wrinkles and bones. Then see how closely your analysis matches the author's interpretation.

AP Photo/Adil Bradlow

Nelson Mandela, sentenced to life in prison for his actions against segregation in South Africa, became the country's first black president in 1994, four years after his early release.

Nelson Mandela

Lines: _____

_____

_____

_____

_____

Bones: _____

_____

_____

_____

Author's interpretation: The face of this great African leader and political survivor is an interesting study of some essential principles of Chinese physiognomy. Indeed, few faces in modern times contain features and characteristics so dramatically different in significance than that of Nelson Mandela. His life is a perfect combination of wealth and poverty, blessings and disasters, fortune and misfortune.

One of the most outstanding features of his face is its deep lines. These lines reveal a lot of the secrets about the fate of this great champion of democracy. As famous as he is, his fate is anything but smooth, largely because the lines in his forehead are broken. From a physiognomic perspective, broken lines in the forehead indicate plenty of hardship and disasters in one's life, including financial difficulty, family trouble, divorce, legal problems, imprisonment, or even a violent death. This is especially the case when the lines are not only broken, but also deep.

Since the forehead stands for the early stages in one's life, we can be sure that Mandela must have come from a hard family background in which his parents were either financially strained, had a bad relationship, were separated or divorced, or one of them died early in his life. In a word, his childhood was simply not happy.

The lines in the forehead also reveal important information about one's entire life, too. Mandela's broken lines almost guaranteed that he would be separated, if not divorced, from his wife for a long period of time. This was realized when he was sentenced to life imprisonment and spent the next twenty-five years behind bars, separated from his ex-wife, Winnie. After he was released in 1990, there already existed some insurmountable gaps in affection and understanding between the couple. Their divorce should have come as no surprise to the world. To be fair, neither is to blame.

The good news for Mandela is that all these disastrous episodes may just be blessings in disguise, so long as he has the willpower to survive. An experienced face reader could see clearly the silver linings

behind his cloudy face even when he was a prisoner. Again, this is revealed first in the lines on his face.

Look at the two long, deep lines that extend from the side of his nose all the way down to his chin, and in good symmetry with both his nose and mouth. These are falins or, literally, lines of authority. Long, deep, and clear falins like these indicate distinct power and authority. Judging by the excellence of his falins, Mandela was born to be a leader endowed with strong power and authority. This has been true for decades, but most significantly in the last stage of his life, since falins are located in the lower portion of a face, which stands for one's old age. It is mainly this pair of falins that not only makes him a classic survivor, but also pushed him to the peak of power. This time not as the president of the African National Congress, but as the president of South Africa.

As if this is not enough to show the rebounding force of fate, he married a devoted woman not long after his divorce. Keep in mind that all these wonderful things occurred to him after he had passed the age of seventy. One cannot help but feel astonished by the delicate arrangement of fate, which has a timing for everything.

Of course, excellent falins alone are not enough to cause all these blessings to happen. Part of the credit should be given to the bones in his face. Look carefully at his forehead and you will notice a pair of symmetrical bones standing out above his eyebrows. These are known as the Sun and Moon bones, another significant indicator of unusual power and authority. His outstanding and protruding cheekbones also contribute to his ascent to supreme power in the country.

Chapter 22

Face Reading Tips

At this point, you should be able to start reading faces so as to better understand yourself and others and to better prepare for upcoming events that will directly affect your future. Since a lot of information has been covered concerning the principles, methods, and various criteria of Chinese face reading, you may be feeling a bit overwhelmed or are just looking for a brief summary of the main points. The following fifteen tips are just that—a general guideline to use when learning and practicing to read faces on your own.

1. **When to read:** Don't read a person's face when he or she is sleepy, angry, depressed, has just had sexual intercourse, or is under the influence of alcohol. Under such circumstances, one's original color and spirit, especially that of the eyes, will be confusing and hard to detect, leading to misinterpretation. Also, don't read a face while you yourself are tired and in low spirits. Nor should you read a face while in the street with many people walking by or in any distracting location. Face reading requires wholehearted concentration on the part of the reader.

2. **Gender:** Make sure that you know the gender of the person being read. That is to say, do not assume or be misled based on the style of dress, hairstyle, or mannerisms of a person. Sometimes these outward enhancements can successfully hide the real gender of a person. This advice may sound ridiculous, but it seems to be a necessary one for the world in which we live today. Knowing the gender is important because of the principle of yin and yang, where the same facial feature, color, or age can have very different meanings for a male and a female. (See chapter 2.)

3. **Artificial alterations:** Find out if any part of the person's face has undergone plastic surgery or any other alterations—practices that have become fairly commonplace nowadays, particularly for the teeth, eyes, and nose as well as the entire face (a face lift). You must be very careful in drawing conclusions on those features that have undergone plastic surgery or any major surgery as well, because they are considered distorted, from a physiognomic point of view. In such cases, a correct analysis cannot be made without the help of additional divination systems such as astrology or numerology.

Minor surgery or injuries, such as scars or having a tooth pulled should not be too much of a concern, so long as the client states clearly what kind of surgery or injury occurred and where. It might be helpful to look at some pictures of the client before the surgery or injury.

Birth defects are indicators of fate and should be read as such in the light of the rules and principles governing individual facial features. For instance, some people are born with a cleft palate, some with eleven toes, and some with only one ear. Personally, I have seen three people born with only one ear. These are, of course, rare exceptions. Nonetheless, they carry significant meanings with them. Thus, a cleft palate indicates that the person has to work very hard in order to make both ends meet in life. Those born with only one ear will likely bring disaster to their spouse, such as divorce, ill health, or an early death due to accident or disease. As for those born with eleven toes, it is an indication that the person can rise to a very high social position but will have a violent ending. Jiang Qing, Mao's wife, was born with eleven toes. She had come very close to acquiring the supreme power in China, but was eventually sentenced to death and committed suicide.

4. **Geographic location:** Know the birthplace of the people you are reading. Are they from the southern part of the country or the northern part, etc. This is an important piece of information because different geographic locations and ethnic backgrounds will have different physiognomic meanings. This goes back to the principle of the five elements and the Five Mountains system. Thus, for someone from the south, the quality of the fore-

head is of primary importance. In contrast, if one is from the north, the quality of one's chin of the face carries greater weight. (Refer to chapters 2 and 3.)

5. **Spirit and color:** Pay special attention to the spirit and color of the person. These dimensions are extremely important to their immediate future, especially the spirit, which should be the first object of study in any face reading. This is because spirit is the dominant indicator of our immediate fate. Of particular importance is the spirit and color of the eyes, nose, and Life Palace. (See chapter 7.)

6. **Three Portions:** Look carefully at the three portions of the face to get a broad picture or a general idea of its significance (Three Portions system). Generally, if the three portions are of equal or similar length, the person is blessed and will have an easy life. (See chapter 3.)

7. **Twelve Palaces:** Use the Twelve Palaces system to get a good idea about the major aspects of the person's life. If time is limited, this method can be a useful way to get a broad reading of a person. Combined with the information of the three por-

tions of a face, you should be able to arrive at general conclusions regarding the major aspects of the person's life and fate. (See chapter 4.)

8.   **Face shape:** Determine if the face completely falls into one of the five basic shapes. If it does, you can draw a number of conclusions from that before moving on to the individual features for more specific details. If the face does not fall completely into any one of the shapes, which is the rule rather than the exception, you'll have to ignore this step or use the face shape that appears the most dominant. (See chapter 5.)

9.   **Man-animal resemblance:** See if the person's face closely resembles one of the animal shapes defined in Appendix A. It is believed that as long as one's face and physique highly resembles that of an animal, that person will have characteristics similar to that animal. Rarely does a person closely match one of the shapes; it is usually the exception rather than the rule. When one does, it indicates that person will be able to ascend to a high position and enjoy honor and wealth in life.

10.   **Feature weight:** Face reading is an art of synthesis and analysis. Of the total weight of a face, the eyes determine 60 percent of our fate, while the nose, eyebrows, ears, and mouth each determine 10 percent of our fate. In other words, whatever the eyes foretell, it outweighs the fate revealed by the other features.

11.   **Unique features:** Pay special attention to the abnormalities rather than the commonalties; in other words, concentrate on what is unique about the person. Above all, it is the individuality that tells the difference between this particular person and the rest of humankind. For instance, does the person have unusually long arms? Are the ears profoundly protruding? Are the eyes especially large? Are the eyebrows very bushy? Is the nose exceptionally long?

12.   **Age:** Make sure that you know the correct age of the person being read. The age is used to help determine the normal color for that person and also in cases where the person only wants to know his or her immediate future. Once this piece of vital information is secured, you can jump directly to the specific facial location assigned to the age of the person (age mapping). Examine this facial location, and that of the next year or so, from the aspect of gender, color, spirit, structure, its

specific physiognomic meaning, and its relation to the rest of the face. This will enable you to draw correct conclusions about the person's current affairs and fate in the near future. (See chapter 5.)

For instance, if the person is forty-eight years old, male or female, you should go directly to the nose tip and give it a careful analysis. (See Figures 5.1 and 5.2, pages 39 and 40.) What is the color like? Are there any lines or moles on it? Is it round, fleshy, and large or small, pointed, and crooked? If the nose tip is big, how about the two wings? Is the nose in balance with the other facial features? Based on the answers to these and other questions, you will be able to tell how well the person is faring at the age of forty-eight in terms of career, family, and financial situation.

13. **Order:** Time permitting, go from one location to another, one feature to another, in a chronological order, based on the age map (basically the order of the chapters in this book). Examine each location and feature carefully and comprehensively, so as to get a complete picture of the fate of a person.

14. **Non-facial features:** Pay attention to the non-facial features of a person: how they walk, sit, speak, laugh, eat and sleep; these all carry some significant message about the personality and fate of the person. Thus, if he or she walks with their hands closely held to the body, he or she is likely to be a cautious and conservative person. If the person sits with their legs set widely apart, he or she is more easy-going, who does not worry about small matters. It would take another book for me to describe in detail the secret language of such non-facial features, so suffice it to say that they are also a part, though a complementary part, of the profound art of Chinese face reading.

15. **Voice:** Of all the non-facial features, the quality of a person's voice is considered the final and finishing touch in a face reading. Fathers of Chinese physiognomy tell us that if the sound one makes is hoarse and husky, one will not travel very far in a career, even if the face is very good.

永美命

Appendix A:
Man-Animal Resemblance

Fathers of face divination believe that the human face and body can resemble various animal shapes. It is their belief that as long as one's face and physique highly resemble those of a certain animal, one will have characteristics similar to that animal. By means of observation and insight, they have drawn several analogies between humans and animals in terms of both personality and fate. If one fits into one of the defined animal shapes, that person will be able to ascend to a high position, and enjoy honor and wealth in one's life. However, one's ending will be different depending on which animal one resembles.

All of the shapes listed below foretell a fate that will enjoy honor and wealth. Honor means a successful career, the honor of successfully passing the imperial examination which typically led to high governmental positions in traditional Chinese society, in which social authority and power belonged to government only. Typically, high government positions were personally appointed by the emperor. Therefore, holding such positions were considered a great honor not only for the position holders, but for their families and ancestors as well.

In modern society, a general manager or CEO can be considered a position of honor, because politics—even at the national level—is so deeply influenced by money nowadays. Wealth simply means money and all money-related properties, but not intellectual or mental wealth.

The following is a list of animal shapes observed by Chinese fathers of physiognomy. They can be applied to men and women and can be used as a stand-alone analysis of one's fate. It should be kept in mind that most people will not fit into one of these shapes. They are more the exception than the rule, further pointing out the high level of honor and position such people hold.

Ape Shape

Ape-shaped people have a round, small face, with round eyes, long arms, and short feet. They walk quickly, and are loud in voice, and gentle in temper. These people will enjoy honor and wealth such as high governmental positions, successful careers, and good income. However, the honor they enjoy is more likely superficial honor rather than real power. That is to say, they do not hold real decision-making power, such as an honorable president of a company or university. The good news is that these people usually enjoy a long, healthy life.

Bear Shape

Bear-shaped people have a square face, broad forehead, high nose bridge, large mouth with thick lips, zigzagged teeth, and a protruding chin. They are fat in body and limbs, and slow in walking and action. When they walk, their hands move only slightly. Their nose tip is big and round, and they have lots of body hair. These people are brave, calculating, and profound in thinking, and can hold high government positions.

Crane Shape

Crane-shaped people are tall and slim, with a small head and a long neck. Their faces are delicate and handsome, with eyebrows that turn downward. They are weak in physique and gentle in temper. They walk in big strides and enjoy vacationing in beautiful places, such as famous summer resorts. Crane-shaped people will hold good social positions. The more famous examples include Li Hongzhan, the premier to the Empress Dowager of the Qing dynasty, and Lu Dongbin, a famous immortal in the Sung dynasty who is said to have attained enlightenment during his life and was therefore able to live over 300 years.

Deer Shape

Deer-shaped people have a broad, high forehead, which seems to have some excess flesh hanging down, a high, straight nose, and dark eyes. They are small in stature but quick in walking with lean, long limbs. They can enjoy a happy and long life and a successful career which brings them fame and authority.

Dog Shape

Dog-shaped people have yellow but sharp eyes (the whites of the eyes appear yellowish), a fire-shaped face, a protruding mouth, and a short temper. They eat a lot but sleep little. These people can rise to high military positions and enjoy material affluence in their middle age, but their ending is not encouraging. There is a good chance that they will die in action or be killed by some violent deed such as a car accident, plane crash, or assassination.

Donkey Shape

These people have a long head and neck, a high and broad forehead, bushy eyebrows that are widely set apart, round but deep eyes, and a broad mouth with thin lips. They can enjoy social honor and material prosperity. Typically, these people are hard working and persistent in their endeavors, but they can be very impatient and short-tempered. This characteristic can distance them from their colleagues, even though they harbor no ill motives for others.

Dove Shape

Dove-shaped people have a round head, narrow forehead, round eyes, red nose, and eyebrows broader at the inside edges. Although they are short, they walk in big strides. These people are able to rise to positions of power in the government. They are ambitious but kind-hearted, energetic, and very efficient at work. They tend to think very highly of themselves, and can get impatient with those around them who are slow performers. Honor and prosperity are not strangers to them, but these things usually do not come to them before the age of forty. Their old age will be peaceful and affluent.

Eagle Shape

Eagle-shaped people have a square head that is round on top. Their nose is pointed at the tip, and sometimes leans toward one side of the face. There is also a bump in the nose bridge. Their eyes often look aslant, and their eyebrows are thin. They walk in a hurried manner. These people can be cruel and narrow-minded. They enjoy benefiting themselves at the expense of others, including their friends. Although in so doing they can rise to high military positions. However, their ending is often as violent and as cruel as their heart.

Elephant Shape

Elephant-shaped people have long eyes, thin eyebrows, small nose, visible teeth, a large build, and a high, outstanding fore-head. They do not sleep much, but they are nevertheless energetic. Typically, these are patient people who are capable of not only hard work, but also taking a longer view of life. In other words, they are not naturally aggressive or competitive. They prefer to have things work out for them naturally, through patience and persistence rather than competition. Their fate will get better and better after middle age, and they expect to live a healthy, long life. They will also have many children and grandchildren.

Fox Shape

Fox-shaped people have a small but round head, low, broad forehead, slim but long eyebrows, small, steady eyes, small nose, flat philtrum, big jaws, and a curved mouth that turns downward at the corners. They are low in voice and have a dark complexion. These people enjoy good social positions, but their honor and wealth are often ill-gained. They are typically calculating, unreliable, unfriendly, and obsessed with benefiting themselves at the expense of others, including their friends.

Goat Shape

Goat-shaped people have a square face with a high, outstanding forehead, flat cheek-bones, curved eyes that turn downward and are more white than black, i.e., with small pupils, and slim eyebrows that look more pale than dark. They can hold positions with real personnel and managerial power, and enjoy social honor as well as material prosperity. Many goat-shaped people are after material comforts and carnal pleasures. In particular, they are very libidinous and will spend a lot of energy satisfying their sexual drive. Not surprisingly, many of them will be caught in sexual scandals during their life, which can ruin their career and family life.

Horse Shape

Horse-shaped people have a long face, high cheekbones, a long, prominent nose, big, round eyes, and a wide mouth with large, loosely spaced teeth. They always look as if they are in deep meditation or sorrow. Even their smile carries a hint of sorrow. These people are clever, able, loyal, and eventually hold positions of great power. Typically, they work close to the emperor and have a good chance at becoming premiers of the nation. Unfortunately, their ending is often tragic and miserable.

Better known examples of horse-shaped people include Kou Zun, a gifted premier in the Song Dynasty; Liu Shaoqi, the president of Communist China; and general Dai Li, the famous—or notorious—head of the secret police for Chiang Kai-shek.

Kou Zun was a genius. He could compose excellent poems as a child. One day his father took him to the highest peak of the famous Hua Mountains in western China. After looking around for a while, he burst into a poem: "One day I climb to the very peak of mountains, standing as high as Mountains Hua. Alas! The red sun is so close to me as I look upwards, but all the white clouds are below me as I look downward." Kou was seven years old when he composed this poem, but his soaring ambition was well illustrated by the images he used in the poem. The red sun refers to the son of Heaven, the emperor, and the white clouds stand for other officials and the people of the country. Kou's ambition was fulfilled eventually. He became the premier to Emperor Shen Zhong, but was ordered to commit suicide by the emperor as a face-saving alternative after he was caught in a major corruption scandal.

Liu Shaoqi (1898–1969) became the second most powerful man in the newly founded People's Republic of China, only to be imprisoned and tortured to death during the Cultural Revolution.

Dai Li (1897–1945), the secret police head for Chiang Kai-shek, also enjoyed the trust of the supreme leader, but was killed in a tragic plane crash in which his body was burned almost beyond recognition.

Leopard Shape

Leopard-shaped people have a broad face with a high forehead, a straight nose, round, protruding, fierce eyes, dark eyebrows, high cheekbones, full chin, and closely set teeth that are largely visible. They will enjoy honor and wealth, but they are cruel and do not give a second thought to killing people. Therefore, they will not enjoy longevity.

Lion Shape

Lion-shaped people have a round head, a broad, high forehead, a bone standing out at the back of the head, thick eyebrows, and large eyes with big, dark pupils, high cheekbones, a low nose bridge, a broad mouth, and a thick beard. These people, both male and female, will hold high social positions and enjoy wealth and prosperity.

Ox Shape

The outstanding characteristics of ox-shaped people include a long face, a bare head with little hair, some excess flesh hanging over the corners of the forehead, a high and straight nose, eyes with some red lines in them, and a slightly narrow chin. They walk slowly as if in deep meditation. These people are capable of persistence and hard work, and can also hold high social positions and live long. However, they tend to be very stubborn. They may seem to work more slowly than others, but their efficiency is nonetheless high.

Parrot Shape

Parrot-shaped people have a long face, broad forehead, small eyes but long eyebrows, a high nose with a round tip, and a small mouth with thick lips. These people are often found to be picky and critical of others. They are opportunistic and can be very tight with their money. There can be no doubt that they are good at managing their own money, but they tend to give the impression of being too clever and shrewd

when dealing with others. Consequently, they are not trusted by others.

Phoenix Shape

Phoenix-shaped people have the following characteristics: the body is slender and long, the three portions of the face are roughly the same length; the forehead is high and beautiful; the ears lie flat against the head with outstanding circles; a high nose with a fleshy and round nose tip; and long, graceful eyes with eyebrows that turn upward at the outer edges. These people are bound to enjoy honor and wealth, coupled with a big family. Chances are that they can hold the position of premier.

Rabbit Shape

Rabbit-shaped people have a small head with a pointed forehead, small eyes that are more black than white, slim eyebrows, a small but angular mouth with rosy lips, small, highly-set ears, and a small nose with rounded tip. These people are friendly, and especially gifted with literary talents. Their fate before the age of thirty will be very uneasy and fluctuating.

Snake Shape

Snake-shaped people have a long face with a greenish complexion, long eyes that are white than black (small pupils), small teeth, a small but long nose, and ears that are wider on top than at the bottom. When they walk, they often zigzag involuntarily, with their eyes looking upward. These people can enjoy wealth and good social position, but their endings are often violent and miserable.

Tiger Shape

Tiger-shaped people have a round head, large eyes, and a short neck. Their face is largely that of a fire type, with its lower portion broader than its upper portion. Their eyebrows are as long as their eyes, and their eyes are big but with red lines. They have a relatively low nose, with the nostrils vaguely visible, and also red lips. Their cheekbones are high, and there seem to be some bones standing out in their Life Palace. They walk in big strides and speak in a loud voice. They eat fast and noisily. When they look at others, they seem to carry an authoritative air bordering on command.

These are people who can hold high social positions and great power, especially military power.

Tortoise Shape

Tortoise-shaped people have small but long heads which are held high and look upward, with a broad forehead, small mouth, closely set teeth, and ears that are wider at the bottom than on top. They often look sanguine in complexion, and take big strides in walking. They will enjoy honor and prosperity.

Unicorn Shape

Unicorn-shaped people have a broad, high forehead, a large mouth, ears that rise above the eyebrows, deep eyes, and bushy eyebrows. They walk in a stately manner. Those people with such a shape will enjoy great honor and wealth.

Appendix B:
The Traditional Wife

Based on the principle of yin and yang and the traditional views of face reading, there are great differences between men and women in what makes an ideal facial feature. A whole set of rules were developed solely for the purpose of reading female faces.

Throughout this book, I have tried to give more modern interpretations of fate for women, to reflect today's changing cultural values. But in this appendix, as a historical aside, I would like to reveal the original interpretations created by the fathers of face reading centuries ago.

The traditional Chinese male who was serious about marrying someone or maintaining a long-

224 — Appendix B

term relationship, was advised to keep in mind the following secrets regarding a woman's face. These secrets have been verified again and again for generations, and are still considered powerful tools when selecting a good, traditional marriage partner.

My focus here will be on the specific features a man was told to look for when choosing a wife, again, from a traditional point of view. Some of the more unique observations made by face reading masters will be interesting and surprising information to many outside the Chinese culture.

Forehead: A good forehead for a woman should be smooth, of medium height, and rounded but not protruding.

While a high, deep forehead is an auspicious sign for a man, it is definitely not recommended for a woman, because such a forehead will bring bad luck to her husband and destroy an otherwise happy family life. Typically, women with high foreheads will fail in their first marriage, ending either in the death of their husbands or divorce.

Eyebrows: The principle of yin and yang states that males should be strong and brave, and females should be weak and gentle. Therefore, thick eyebrows on a woman are not, according to traditional theory, a good feature to have since they indicate an inability to be a good housewife and that she will bring bad luck to her husband. The

woman is considered strong, sexy, ambitious, almost dominating, and can be very successful in a career, but is viewed as having an unhappy or troubled family life.

Traditionally, females with thin eyebrows are delicate and gentle in temperament, more submissive and lovable, and stand a greater chance of being good wives and having a happy family life. There is no connection between thin eyebrows and weak health as there is for a male.

A woman's eyebrows are more expressive than those of a man, especially in terms of her sexuality. The thicker and more curved the eyebrows are, the more sexually vital the woman is.

While a broad space between the eyebrows is indicative of a high government position for a man, such a space on a female face is an indication of a lewd woman, although she may have a good career and happy childhood.

While a narrow space between the eyebrows is inauspicious for a man, it can be a good sign for a woman, for it indicates that she is a good sexual partner and more conservative in the family budgeting.

Eyes: Good female eyes are graceful, gentle, and dark, with large pupils.

"Those with big eyes are hardly wicked." "There is no good woman with eyes that look aslant at others." These are considered important rules for judging a woman. For one thing, large-eyed women are more extroverted in character, more emotional and outspoken. They are open-minded and more accessible than small-eyed women. If a woman looks aslant at others, she must have wicked intentions.

Protruding eyes are a sign of a widow early in life. Such women usually have profound feeling toward their husbands, preferring to remain single after the death of their husbands.

Long eyelashes signify artistic tastes and talents. These women are often skillful at music, painting, and cooking. Their chances of success in these fields are very high. Women with short eyelashes can be very skillful in practical affairs, but they are often shrewd and calculating.

Eyes of different sizes indicate jealousy and cunning. The relationship between her parents is often bad, a fact which makes her all the more yearning for lasting and possessive love. She tends to exhibit strong jealous reactions in romantic affairs. If found competing with another woman for a man's affections, she may choose to kill her romantic competitor at the cost of her own life.

Nose: A woman's nose is her "husband star." Her social position and happiness depends largely on the man she marries, therefore, the nose can hardly be underestimated. If her nose is auspicious, she will marry a loving husband, have a secure livelihood, and enjoy family life, if not extreme wealth. Hence the saying that there is no widow with a round and fleshy nose.

While a high nose bridge is an auspicious sign for wealth and high position for a man, such a nose is not desirable for a woman. This characteristic traditionally means too strong of a personality, something not typically desirable for a harmonious marriage.

A good nose for a woman is one that has a bright, fleshy, and round nose tip, unbiased, with a smooth bridge, which is not too prominent, coupled with full wings and invisible nostrils. Such a nose will ensure her of a happy marriage, secure financial provisions, and a good career.

An inauspicious nose is one with a pointed tip, a broken bridge, marred with moles or lines, or biased to one side. A pointed nose tip indicates bad luck for her husband and her own wealth. A broken bridge indicates ill health for her and her husband. Moles on the nose signify disease, and a biased nose indicates bankruptcy and loss of money.

Ears: A woman's ears can tell a lot about her sexuality. Many face readers hold that the structure of a woman's ears reflects the structure of her vagina, specifically the size of her ear door. It is said that if the ear door is narrow, her vagina is also narrow; if the ear door is wide, her vagina is wide, too.

Also indicative of her sexuality is the color of her ears. Face reading masters hold that the redder a woman's ears are compared to her face, the stronger her sexuality.

Earlobes partly determine her husband's fate and partly determine her own sexuality. The bigger and fuller the earlobes, the more likely she will marry a good husband and bring good luck to him, and the more sexually vital and capable she will be.

Cheekbones: Good cheekbones for a woman are flat, bright, with no lines or moles grown on them.

While high, protruded cheekbones are desirable for a man because they indicate power and authority, such cheekbones are not recommended for a woman. This is because high cheekbones for a woman mean disaster to her husband and children. Most likely, women with high, protruding cheekbones will marry more than once, and they will encounter danger during childbirth, which may very likely end in a miscarriage. Such a woman is hot tempered, with a strong desire to compete and control, which can often result in conflict in a marriage.

If protruding cheekbones are coupled with protruding eyes, the woman will marry at least three times in her life. This is inauspicious because traditional Chinese women consider multiple marriages a great misfortune.

Philtrum: Known as the Renzhong in Chinese physiognomy as well as Chinese acupuncture, the philtrum is symbolic of a woman's womb, the reproductive organ. According to the fathers of face reading, a good philtrum should be deep, long, and unbiased. Such a philtrum will ensure the delivery of healthy, promising children.

On the other hand, if the philtrum is short, flat, narrow, or biased toward one side, the woman will have difficulty conceiving and, especially, a difficult delivery. Even if she has children, they are not likely to be good and filial.

If a woman's philtrum is wider on top than at the bottom, it is a sign of hardship in life.

If a woman's philtrum is wider at the bottom, it is a sign that her luck will improve as she gets older.

As to moles found in the philtrum, interpretation varies depending on the exact location of the moles. If a mole is located in the upper part of the philtrum, it indicates fertility. If it appears in the middle of the philtrum, it indicates divorce. If it is found in the lower part of the philtrum, it speaks of adultery and a loose character. If there are two moles in the philtrum, it is a sign of giving birth to twin babies.

If a horizontal line appears in the philtrum as a woman smiles, it is another indication of adultery. It is observed that this line can also show up if she has had excessive sex.

Hair growing on a woman's philtrum indicates trouble in marriage and possibly divorce, as well as sour relations with family members and solitude in old age.

If a triangle appears where the philtrum borders on the upper lip of the mouth, it is a sign of having more sons than daughters.

If a semicircle appears where the philtrum borders on the upper lip of the mouth, it is an indication of having more daughters than sons.

Mouth: An auspicious female mouth is considered to be round, small, with thick, red lips turning upward at the corners when open. Asian men think that small-mouthed women are gentle, careful, conservative in sexual relations, and capable of taking good care of their husbands and children—all desirable qualities in a good wife. Such a mouth ensures a good, long, and harmonious relationship with a husband. Thin, pale lips mean a cool relationship with her spouse.

Traditionally, Asian men think that women with small mouths are gentle, careful, conservative in sexual relations, and capable of taking good care of their husbands and children—all desirable qualities in a wife. Such a mouth is said to ensure a good, long, and harmonious relationship with her husband.

Females with large, square mouths are generally more active, energetic, independent, romantic, and capable than someone with a small mouth. Typically, women with large mouths will have a hard time finding a husband, although they tend to have many boyfriends. Marriage is not easy and happy for them for the large mouth indicates that they will bring harm to their husbands and families, dooming them to failure and frustration in relationships and marriage. This is the thing least desired in a woman in traditional Chinese society.

Another common belief is that a large mouth on a woman means "devouring her husband," while a large mouth for a man means "delicious food everywhere." Of course, this is an exaggeration. What it really means is that a large mouth on a woman can bring bad luck to her husband. Typically, she will have many boyfriends in life, even after marriage. This is especially the case when not only the mouth is large, but the lips are thick as well. The formula is that the thicker the lips, the sexier the woman, and vice versa. Such women are said to have a strong natural desire for sex.

Fathers of face reading also hold that the size of a woman's vagina can determine to a large extent whether the sexual life of the couple is harmonious and satisfactory. In other words, the size of her mouth directly reflects the size of her vagina: the bigger the mouth, the broader the vagina, and vice versa. From a sexual viewpoint, the larger the vagina, the harder it will be for the couple's sexual life to be happy and satisfactory. As a result, both partners may seek additional sexual adventures outside of wedlock in order to satisfy their own unfilled sexual appetites. On the other hand, a smaller vagina can make both partners more sensitive to sexual stimulation during the intercourse, resulting in greater satisfaction for both.

A woman's mouth also indicates what kind of children she will have. A good mouth indicates good children, while a bad mouth means having bad (dishonorable) children or children dying young.

Teeth: Teeth indicate the type of relationship between her and her husband. White, clean teeth signify a good, harmonious relationship, whereas yellow or dark teeth indicate just the opposite.

A woman's teeth can also tell something about her sexuality. If teeth are very large, the woman will be very energetic and sexually demanding. However, her sentiment is hardly as delicate as those with small teeth. Crooked teeth indicate jealousy and trouble in childbearing.

Chin: The chin is considered more important to a woman than to a man, just like the forehead is more important to a man than to a woman.

A good female chin is round, thick, large, preferably doubled, and protruding. Such a chin indicates happiness, and longevity. Women with such a chin are found to be devoted to love and family.

A triangular or pointed chin indicates that she is stern in appearance, but kind at heart. A rectangular chin signifies a stubborn character. A pointed chin means she will have a very lonely old age, either because her husband dies, or because she is divorced, or because she is deserted by her children.

Skin: While white or pale skin is considered the beautiful tone for an Asian woman, it is not the auspicious color. If a woman's skin is too white, her character will be too strong and uncompromising. Therefore, fathers of face divination tell us that the best color for a wife is tenderly yellow. A dark skin color on an Asian woman is a sign of loose character and the possibility of divorce.

Hair: In Chinese medicine, sperm is considered the basis for a man's life, while blood is considered the basis of a woman's life. Since hair is thought of as the expression of blood, it bears special meaning for females.

Desirable hair for a woman should be black, lustrous, soft, thick, and long. Again, bear in mind the distinct Chinese background of face reading. Women with such hair have sufficient blood energy, and they will enjoy good health and longevity, capable of delivering healthy babies. At the same time, they can bring honor and good luck to their husbands and children.

If a woman's hair is short, dry, and coarse, it indicates a bad temper and disaster for the husband. Most likely, she will marry more than once, and her marriages will not be happy. She will also have to double her efforts in order to make both ends meet.

Physique: While being slender is conventionally considered a sign of beauty for a woman, it is not recommended by Chinese physiognomy, which considers such a woman as too weak and incapable of hard work. Instead, it holds that a good physique for a woman is one that is plump, with fleshy buttocks. It is observed that such a woman with a full back and fleshy shoulders and buttocks can give birth to good children and that she will benefit from her children in old age.

Appearance: A woman should have a kind, smiling face. Such a face indicates that she has or will have a loving husband. On the contrary, if she assumes an angry, fierce appearance, she will have a hard time living with a man. Fathers of Chinese physiognomy read such a face as detrimental to her husband and children, because it indicated a woman who is narrow-minded and often harbors evil intentions.

永美命

Appendix C:
A Traditional Husband

Finding a good husband has been the single greatest and most challenging project for traditional Chinese women. Until recently, the popular belief has been that a woman becomes honorable and rich all because of her husband, and that to marry a man is to find a livelihood.

While society has undergone dramatic changes since then, and the social position of women has been significantly enhanced, it still remains a challenging and frustrating project for many women to find a good husband. It is worthwhile, therefore, for a woman serious about marrying someone or maintaining a long-term relationship to keep in mind the following ancient secrets regarding a man's face.

This body of knowledge has been verified again and again for generations, and can be powerful tools in your hand when coming to select a good marriage or relational partner. It could save you a lot of time and trouble in the end, and at no cost to you.

My focus will be on specific values governing the choice of a husband from a traditional Chinese woman's point of view. Admitting that women may have different preferences and priorities in this regard, I am assuming that most of them want a husband or partner who is loyal, loving, and kind-hearted, who cares about her happiness, and is a good provider for the family. How can you find such a man from a vast sea of men? I would like to provide you with the following ancient secrets.

Eyes: Eyes are the windows of the mind through which we can see how one thinks and behaves. The eyes of a good husband should be gentle and bright, and slightly curving upward at the outer corners. He will not look aslant at others. Avoid triangular eyes, peach flower eyes, and drunken eyes. Triangular eyes mean, among other things, the great possibility that he will meet with a violent and sudden death. A man with peach blossom eyes is extremely disloyal in love, while a man with drunken eyes is irresponsible toward his wife.

Mouth: The mouth of a good husband should be thick and wide, with red lips that curve upward at the corners. If his mouth is wide and square, his appearance is mild and gentle, and he prefers quiet times to social events, avoids talking about romantic and pornographic affairs, but is reticent in speech and laughter. Such a man will be loyal to his wife in love, and care a lot about her happiness.

On the other hand, if his mouth is small, he will be too stingy and cautious to be of a masculine manner. If the lips are thin and dark, he must be a cruel person.

Nose: A man's nose is not only his "wife star," but also his Wealth Palace. Generally speaking, the bigger the nose, the more capable he is in making money. At the same time, fathers of face reading have discerned that the size of the nose is directly proportional to the size of the penis. In other words, the bigger the nose, the bigger his penis, and vise versa. If a woman seeks wealth and sexual satisfaction from a man, she should pay special attention to this facial feature.

If the nose is biased toward either side, it indicates that the man harbors evil intentions and will likely die a violent death.

Spouse Palaces: The Spouse Palaces are located at the outer corners of the eyes. These are places where a man's personality, his attitude toward romance and love, and the quality of his family life are revealed. If a man's Spouse Palaces are full, fleshy, and bright, uncovered or only slightly covered by lines, with no moles on them, he will be a loyal and affectionate husband.

Eyebrows and cheekbones: If a woman considers herself strong and independent, she should look for a man with thin, curved eyebrows, kind and handsome eyes, flat cheekbones, and a narrow space between the eyebrows. He will most likely have a gentle temper and be a husband who is willing to share control in the marriage. Such a match has a great chance of success if you can avoid head-on conflicts.

Forehead: The forehead is the emphasis of a male's face. A high, broad, and protruding forehead means extraordinary ability and ambition for a man. He will have a successful career sooner or later. On the contrary, a low, narrow forehead covered by hair indicates professional frustration and violent death.

福 Glossary

Doctrine of the Middle Way: One of the cornerstones of Confucianism advocates that we adhere to the Middle Way in our behavior and conduct. The Middle Way is interpreted as a lack of bias, prejudice, and excess. For, as Confucius maintained, too much is as bad as too little, neither of which will last long because both will cause harm and damage, not only to others, but also to ourselves. Only the Middle Way, which is the midpoint or compromise between two extremes, can endure (similar to the principle of harmony and balance). Thus, a short face with a long nose is not in accordance with the doctrine of the Middle Way and, therefore, is not a very auspicious sign.

Instead, a short face with a short nose is considered auspicious.

feng shui: Technically known as geomancy, feng shui is a unique product of Chinese culture that has a history of 3,000 years. Literally the "wind" and the "water," feng shui seeks to design residential, commercial buildings, and tombs in such a way that maximizes the harmony among the macrocosms—that is, among heaven, earth, and humans—so that the residents of the building will benefit from the natural force of the environment, rather than punished by it. The understanding is that the environment has a great impact on our well-being and fortune. Feng shui is an involved, complex subject that draws heavily upon the Taoist theories of yin and yang and the five elements system.

five elements: The five elements in Chinese philosophy and medicine refer to water, fire, wood, metal, and earth. These elements, especially their relationships of mutual creation and mutual destruction, lie at the core of Chinese culture and health care. The five elements are thought to be the raw materials of the universe and everything in it. Human beings, regarded as the microcosm of universe, possess all of these elements. The relationships among the elements signify the growth and development of life and disease, and the five element system is widely used in medical diagnosis and fortune telling. This system is used in the determination of facial color.

Five Mountains system: In China, there are famous mountains in the eastern, western, central, southern, and northern parts of the country. In physiognomy, these mountains correspond to the following features of a face: left and right cheekbones, nose, forehead, and chin. Since these mountains are noted for their height, it is held that the representative facial features also be high and outstanding, so that all these features face each other. If this is the case, one will have a very lucky life and enjoy honor, wealth, and prosperity. This system is used in the determination of facial color.

I Ching: One of the oldest and most significant classic books in China. It is regarded as the source of traditional Chinese culture. It explains in detail the theory and implications of yin and yang, the trigrams, as well as the origin of the universe and how man is related to the universe. Its original purpose was to aid in fortune telling for both individuals and the entire nation. Later generations have found it very useful in almost all fields of human endeavors, from medicine to geomancy, from warfare to politics, from astronomy to business. This is because the principles contained in the book are universal truths.

physiognomy: Another name for the Chinese art of face reading, which has a history of more than 3,000 years. Invented by the Taoist immortal Gui Gu-Tze, physiognomy is a highly involved subject that classifies facial and bodily features into dozens of classes, each of which possess some specific characteristics and properties. By means of such understanding, an expert of face reading can tell the personality and fortune of people just by looking at them, without even knowing them.

qi energy: Qi is an encompassing concept in Chinese medicine, philosophy, and, indeed, the entire traditional Chinese culture. Broadly, qi can be defined as life energy on which depends life itself and the universe. The stronger the qi one possesses, the stronger will be one's immune system, the healthier one will be, and the sooner one will recover from disease. As such, the conservation, promotion, and circulation of qi becomes one of the central themes in traditional Chinese health care and medicine, as well in Chinese philosophy.

reincarnation: A central belief of Buddhism and Taoism that on death the souls of men and animals pass into new bodies of the same or different species. This process continues over and over again, and serves as nature's punishment or reward for one's behavior in the prior life.

Tao: The essence of Taoism. According to the teachings of Lao Tze and Chuang Tze, Tao, or the Way of Nature, is the source and supreme, ultimate principle of the whole universe, of which humankind is a part.

Three Portions system: Chinese physiognomy roughly divides a human face into three portions: the upper portion, the middle portion, and the lower portion. The upper portion consists of the forehead, the middle portion extends downward from the eyebrows to the end of the nose, and the lower portion extends from the philtrum to the chin. These three portions correspond to the three stages of life: childhood and youth, middle age, and old age. Therefore, the quality of each portion determines the quality of life during that stage of life.

Twelve Palaces: Chinese face reading identifies twelve locations on the face that signify twelve different aspects of life. These locations are called palaces to show their special importance. For instance, the Wealth Palace reveals the fate of our financial situation; the Brother/Sister Palace tells us how many siblings we have or will have; and the Career Palace reveals information about our career path.

yin and yang: This pair of polarities stands for almost everything and every phenomenon in the universe. Broadly speaking, yin is the principle realized on earth, while yang is the principle realized in heaven. Individually, both polarities command a bizarre constellation of objects, properties, and phenomena. Yin stands for the earth, the female, moon, night, benevolence, darkness, softness, water, etc. Yang represents the heavens, the male, sun, day, righteousness, brightness, hardness, fire, etc. It is in their combination, interrelation, and interdependence that everything in the universe has, and will, come into being, including the universe itself. There is wide application of the yin and yang theory in human affairs, including traditional Chinese medicine and health care, physics, biology, and military and political sciences.

Bibliography

Bodhidharma Dharma. *Dharma on Five Senses.*
A.D. 400.

Chen, Meng-lei. *Shen hsiang chuan pien* (A
Complete Collection of Divine Physiognomy).
Taipei, Taiwan: National Press, 1959.

Chen Tuan. *Divine Physiognomy of Ma Yi* (in
Chinese). Hong Kong: Hsing Sheng
Publications, 1948.

_____. *A Complete Collection of Divine
Physiognomy* (in Chinese). 1590.

_____. *On the Heart and Face* (in Chinese).
1130.

Chen Zhao. *The True Principles of Physiognomy* (in Chinese). 1788.

Evans, Elizabeth Cornelia. *Physiognomics in the Ancient World*. Philadelphia: American Philosophical Society, 1969.

Gui Gu-Tze. *Xiang Bian Wei Mang*. 250 B.C.

Lao, Jun. *Yue Bo Dong Zhong Ji*. Collected in Ssu Ku Chuan Shu, Vol. 810, compiled by Zhu Jianmin. Taipei, Taiwan: Taiwan Commercial Press, 1986.

Lee, Siow Mong. *The Chinese Art of Studying the Head, Face and Hands*. Malaysia: Pelanduk Publications,1989.

Lu Dongbin. *Divine Physiognomy of Lu Dongbin* (in Chinese). 850 A.D.

Rivers, Christopher. *Face Value: Physiognomical Thought and the Legible Body in Marivaux, Lavater, Balzac, Gautier and Zola*. University of Wisconsin Press, 1994.

Sima, Qian. *Shi Chi* (Annals of History). Nanjing, China: Jinlin Press, 1866.

Song, Qiqiu. *Yu Guan Zhao Shen Ju*. Collected in *Ssu Ku Chuan Shu*, vol. 810, compiled by Zhu Jianmin. Taipei, Taiwan: Taiwan Commercial Press, 1986.

Wang, Pu. *Tai Ching Shen Jian*. Collected in *Ssu Ku Chuan Shu*, vol. 810, compiled by Zhu Jianmin. Taipei, Taiwan: Taiwan Commercial Press, 1986.

Weng, Naichien. *Ancient Chinese Art of Face Reading* (in Chinese). Wuhan, China: Wuhan Industrial University Press, 1993.

Yuan Liuzhuan. *Divine Physiognomy of Liuzhuan* (in Chinese). Kowloon, Hong Kong: Chen Hsiang-chi Book Store, 1953.

Yuan Tiangangg. *Gui Jian Ding Ming Wu Xing Xiang Shu*. A.D. 630.

Zen Guofan. *Bing Jian*. 1850.

Zhang, Xingjian. *Ren Lun Da Tung Hu*. 1185. Collected in *Ssu Ku Chuan Shu*, vol. 810, compiled by Zhu Jianmin. Taipei, Taiwan: Taiwan Commercial Press, 1986.

福 Index

☾ REACH FOR THE MOON

Llewellyn publishes hundreds of books on your favorite subjects! To get these exciting books, including the ones on the following pages, check your local bookstore or order them directly from Llewellyn.

ORDER BY PHONE

- Call toll-free within the U.S. and Canada, 1-800-THE MOON
- In Minnesota, call (651) 291-1970
- We accept VISA, MasterCard, and American Express

ORDER BY MAIL

- Send the full price of your order (MN residents add 7% sales tax) in U.S. funds, plus postage & handling to:

  Llewellyn Worldwide
  P.O. Box 64383, Dept. K433-2
  St. Paul, MN 55164–0383, U.S.A.

POSTAGE & HANDLING

(For the U.S., Canada, and Mexico)

- $4.00 for orders $15.00 and under
- $5.00 for orders over $15.00
- No charge for orders over $100.00

We ship UPS in the continental United States. We ship standard mail to P.O. boxes. Orders shipped to Alaska, Hawaii, The Virgin Islands, and Puerto Rico are sent first-class mail. Orders shipped to Canada and Mexico are sent surface mail.

International orders: Airmail—add freight equal to price of each book to the total price of order, plus $5.00 for each non-book item (audio tapes, etc.).

Surface mail—Add $1.00 per item.

Allow 2 weeks for delivery on all orders.
Postage and handling rates subject to change.

DISCOUNTS

We offer a 20% discount to group leaders or agents. You must order a minimum of 5 copies of the same book to get our special quantity price.

FREE CATALOG

Get a free copy of our color catalog, *New Worlds of Mind and Spirit*. Subscribe for just $10.00 in the United States and Canada ($30.00 overseas, airmail). Many bookstores carry *New Worlds*—ask for it!

Visit our web site at www.llewellyn.com for more information.

Chinese Numerology

The Way to Prosperity & Fulfillment

Richard Webster

Chinese Numerology teaches the original system of numerology which is still practiced throughout the East, and from which Chinese astrology, feng shui and the I Ching were all derived. Chinese numerology as presented here is the quickest and easiest method of character analysis ever devised. Early into the book, you will be able to build a complete picture of a person just as soon as you know his or her birthdate. By the end of the book, you will be able to erect and interpret numerology charts in three different ways. With this knowledge, you will know more about yourself and the motivations of others. You'll also know when to move ahead and when to hold back in different areas of your life.

- Draw a numerology chart in a matter of seconds and be able to interpret it accurately
- Is this a money year? A good year to get married? Discover the future trends in you life by looking at your personal years, months and days
- Uncover your compatibility with another person using an easy technique that has never been published before
- Find out which famous people share the same numerology as you
- Determine whether you have an arrow of loneliness, losses or confusion in your chart and what to do about it
- Learn three interlocking systems of numerology, all of which evolved from the days of Wu of Hsia in ancient China

Includes solar-lunar conversion tables to the year 2000

1-56718-804-4, 260 pp., 7 x 10 $12.95

Prices subject to change without notice.
To order, call 1-800 THE MOON